Breakthrough to the Big League

The Story of Jackie Robinson

AMERICAN
★
CAVALCADE

Breakthrough to the Big League

The Story of Jackie Robinson

★

JACKIE ROBINSON
&
ALFRED DUCKETT

MARSHALL CAVENDISH
CORPORATION

GREY CASTLE PRESS

Published by Grey Castle Press, Lakeville, Connecticut.

Marshall Cavendish Edition, North Bellmore, New York.

Published in large print by arrangement with Harper & Row, Publishers, Inc.

Printed in the USA.

Library of Congress Cataloging-in-Publication Data

Robinson, Jackie, 1919–1972.
   Breakthrough to the big league : the story of Jackie Robinson / by Jackie Robinson and Alfred Duckett.
      p.   cm. — (American cavalcade)
   Reprint. Originally published : New York : Harper & Row, 1965.
   Includes bibliographical references and index.
   Summary: An autobiography of the baseball star who was the first black player to be accepted by a major league team.
      ISBN 1-55905-094-2
      1. Robinson, Jackie, 1919–1972—Juvenile literature.   2. Baseball players—United States—Biography—Juvenile literature.   3. Large type books. [1. Robinson, Jackie, 1919–1972.   2. Baseball players.   3. Afro-Americans—Biography.   4. Large type books.]   I. Duckett, Alfred.   II. Title.   III. Series.
   [GV865.R6A3. 1991]
   92—dc20
   [796.357'092]
   [B]   90-48588
                                                                       CIP
                                                                       AC

ISBN 1-55905-094-2
      1-55905-100-0 (set)

Photo Credits:
Cover: UPI/Bettmann Newsphotos
AP/Wide World—pgs. 55, 81, 140, 154, 165
National Baseball Library, Cooperstown, NY—pgs. 9, 33
UPI/Bettmann Newsphotos—pgs. 27 (top), 107
UCLA—pg. 27 (bottom)

Contents

★

1

I Meet Old Man Jim Crow

IT SHOULD HAVE BEEN ONE of the happiest evenings of my life—and it was. Yet I sat at the center of the head table of the banquet, trying unsuccessfully to conceal the fact that I was crying.

Tears were springing to my eyes so rapidly that it was almost impossible for me to distinguish the individual faces of any of the five or six hundred people seated at tables in front of me and on either side of the banquet room. I wanted to see each and every one of them that night in the Starlight Roof of New York's Waldorf-Astoria Hotel. I knew there were many good friends at those tables.

The dinner was being held in my honor on the evening of July 20, 1962. Three days later I would become a member of the Baseball Hall of Fame. I would be the first black player to win American baseball's highest reward.

The tears, of course, were happy tears. They

were also the kind of tears you can't hold back when good memories begin crowding into your mind. Such memories were coming to me as speaker after speaker addressed the audience and talked about the way I had become the first black to play baseball in the American major leagues.

At the microphone someone read a telegram from President Kennedy. Governor Rockefeller and Dr. Ralph Bunche were among the distinguished guests who sat on the dais.

I loved everybody in that room.

I had a special feeling for eight people there who had deeply influenced my life. It was the first time all eight of them had been together with me at an important event in my life.

Sitting on the dais with me were my wife, Rachel; my mother, Mallie Robinson; and Branch Rickey, the man who gave me my big break in major league baseball.

At one of the front tables were my three children, Jackie Jr., Sharon, and David; and Zellee Isum, Rae's mother.

At another table was Bill Black, the man who had built the big Chock Full O'Nuts Corporation out of a single store and who gave me my big break in business after I left baseball.

The tears were still coming. What made it worse was that it was now time for me to go to the

Jackie Roosevelt Robinson, the first black ever to play on a major league team, was inducted into the Baseball Hall of Fame on July 23, 1962.

microphone to accept a plaque and say a few words of acknowledgment. I could say only a few words. My voice was trembling and I felt too grateful and too happy to try to make a speech.

I didn't get much sleep that night after we got back to our home in Connecticut. My mind was too busy with the excitement of the dinner. I lay in my bed, looking up at the ceiling, thinking of so many wonderful things that had happened to a poor boy born of parents who were almost slaves in the South. I thought back to the days when I was a kid, growing up in California. . . .

Extra, extra! Read all about it.

It was Saturday night in Pasadena. I was standing on the corner of one of that community's busiest streets, desperately trying to attract the attention of some passer-by who would buy my last copy of the Los Angeles *Examiner.* When you're a kid selling newspapers, sometimes it seems you'll never be able to get rid of that last one. You have to sell most of your papers before you begin to make a profit. So selling that last paper means a lot.

I was in my early teens but I was as determined as any big businessman to make some money every day. Every penny would count in helping my mother carry the burden of raising five kids—my three brothers, my sister, and me—with no husband to help her.

I realized very early in life what troubles my mother had seen. I was a kid in a hurry to help her. It hurt me to see her getting up out of her bed before the sun came up so she could get breakfast for us and go out to do domestic work. It hurt me to see her come dragging home, bone-weary from scrubbing floors and ironing clothes. One of these days I wanted to fix it so she could stay home and do all the things I knew she'd love to do in her own house. I was impatient to grow up so I could really help her.

I didn't feel this way because my mother appeared unhappy. On the contrary, she never complained and usually put on a cheerful front for us. She used the fragments of time left to her to do what she could to make our home life the best it could possibly be.

I had become accustomed to seeing her come home, bringing a piece of cake or something the people she worked for would allow her to take. At times when she worked for someone with a son my age, I was really lucky. I might get a cast-off suit or a pair of shoes that fit me.

Sometimes I had bitter thoughts about my father. He had deserted my mother and the five of us, back there where I was born on a small farm near Cairo, Georgia.

Even though slavery had been ended for well over forty years when my mother and father were married in 1909, many blacks in the South were living under a new kind of slavery almost as bad as the old. They were physically free, but they lived in economic bondage. They worked on large plantations in exchange for living quarters which were little more than shacks. They received whatever wages their bosses wanted to pay. My father, Jerry Robinson, had been one of those half-free, half-slave unfortunates. Like many others, he accepted this miserable way of life because he did not believe life held anything better for him.

My mother was different. When Christmas of 1909 came, the year my parents were married, my father had come home with fifteen dollars in his pocket. This was not even money he had earned. It was an advance he had been forced to borrow on his pay for the following year. Of this, he gave my mother five dollars to take care of holiday needs.

My mother told my father he was doing the wrong thing by not standing up for his rights. Here he was, a strong, intelligent man, working the year round for twelve dollars a month. In order to survive he had to continue to live in debt. My mother urged my father to demand a half interest in the crops he cultivated for his boss. My father was afraid to do this. Too often he had seen black workers thrown off the land because they had asked for more. My mother finally convinced my father that he should take a chance. She believed that a human being has to stand up for his rights and that even if he suffers for it, God will look out for him in the long run.

My mother's faith proved justified a few years after that miserable Christmas. My father finally agreed to take her advice. He approached his employers and was amazed when his request was granted. After that things were a lot better for him and his rapidly growing family. We had more food, better clothes, and—most important to my mother—more self-respect.

The improved conditions lasted only a few years. One day my father went away, saying he was going to Memphis to seek another job. He never came back. My mother was left with the job of bringing up five of us. I was the youngest, born on the last day of January, 1919. There was Edgar, ten, Frank, eight, Mack, six—and my sister Willa Mae, four. I was sixteen months old when my mother decided that there was no hope for us in the Deep South. She was an uneducated woman but she was wise enough to refuse to accept things as they were. She was courageous enough to venture to seek a new life in some other part of the country. Her brother, Burton, was living in California. He promised to send what little money he could spare. My mother decided to sell our few possessions and take us to California.

Of course I was too young to be affected by the hardship of the long nights and days of travel from Cairo, Georgia, to Pasadena. But when I was old enough to understand what my mother had done, the trip seemed dramatic and romantic to me. I compared it with the journeys the pioneers made when they traveled West in covered wagons, accepting discomfort and danger in order to try to establish a new life for themselves. I could just imagine what my mother had gone through, almost penniless, with five small, restless, hungry children on her hands. She must have wondered if she had done the right thing, and when the days turned into nights as we rode that bus, she must have become frightened trying to figure out whether our future would be bright or dark.

Back in Cairo good friends had warned my mother that it wouldn't be easy, trying to start a new life. It wasn't. At first we had to live with my Uncle Burton. Naturally quarters were crowded, but my uncle wanted to save my mother the necessity of paying rent. He wanted to give her a chance to get on her feet. My mother didn't waste any time. She began to take in washing and ironing and soon we moved into an apartment of our own. We couldn't keep the place long. The hours my mother worked and the money she made didn't balance the cost of clothing and feeding five growing kids. We had to give up the apartment and go back to my uncle's.

Then mother made another decision which took almost as much daring as she had shown in leaving Georgia. She would buy her own house and rent to others. It must have taken seemingly endless hours of ironing and washing and some almost miraculous scrimping and saving for her to carry out her resolve. But she was determined to succeed. We finally moved into a home which we could look forward to owning and where we had more room.

Even in our new home we couldn't always afford two meals a day. Plain bread and sweet water were often considered a treat. My mother was still getting up in the dark just before dawn and leaving the house to go to work for people who were lucky enough to be able to hire servants.

Even though she couldn't always give us enough to eat, my mother was determined that we should not starve for education. She was also determined that we should grow up with a sense of religious responsibility. Most important to her was the desire to keep the family together.

It has always seemed a miracle to me that Mallie Robinson managed to achieve all three of these aims. We got our schooling. I started going to school by sitting in a sandbox. I was too young to be left home by myself. The other Robinson children had to go to school and my mother had to go to work. So Willa Mae, who was three years older than I, took charge of the problem. Every morning Willa Mae took me to school. She would leave me to play in a sandbox just outside the building. I found ways to amuse myself while Willa Mae and my brothers were in class. But I was pretty happy when lunch and dismissal hours arrived.

Growing up in our family was mainly a happy experience. Even if we didn't have many advantages financially, we had wonderful times together. All of us were devoted to Willa Mae, the only girl. She was such an openly affectionate person that you just couldn't help liking her. My oldest brother, Edgar, kept us in a state of constant fear. He was so reckless on his skates and with his cherished bicycle. I sometimes think he took so many chances because it secretly delighted him to see that we were so concerned.

I loved everyone in my family, but there was something special about my brother Mack. A superb athlete, Mack was my boyhood hero. He was one of the fastest track stars in our school. Mack vindicated my faith in him one proud day in 1936 when the entire Robinson family danced and shouted with delight on learning from a radio broadcast that our Mack had finished second to Jesse Owens in Berlin in the Olympic 200-meter.

Perhaps one of the reasons I idolized Mack was that I too had an early love for all kinds of sports. When I was eight years old, my mother made me a delightful ball of old woolen socks. I spent many long hours with the ball and a stick.

Pasadena, where we lived, is a lovely suburb of Los Angeles. Yet picturesque as Pasadena was, it was there, as a youngster, that I first began to learn about the ugliness of racial hatred. I couldn't help sensing the atmosphere of unpleasantness that we encountered when we moved into an all-white neighborhood and the residents there entered into an unsuccessful conspiracy to buy us out or to make our lives so miserable that we would want to leave. Once a little girl neighbor began calling me ''nigger, nigger, nigger'' as I was sweeping the sidewalk. I called back that she was a ''cracker,'' a word which, to a white Southerner, is as contemptuous as any insult. Her father rushed out of the house and we began throwing rocks at each other until his wife came out and broke up the battle.

Even before I went to high school and college I resolved not to take insults without retaliating. Growing up in Pasadena, I encountered many situations which I considered unjust. I remember going to the YMCA and being told that blacks were allowed to use the facilities of the Y only on a certain day of the week. I'm glad to say that this kind of unchristian practice has disappeared from our YMCA and YWCA setups everywhere— except in some Southern communities; but that is the way it was when I was a youngster in Pasadena.

I remember going to the municipal swimming pool and being told that Tuesday was the day for the black kids. I remember going to the local movie house and being ushered to a special section on the right side of the theater or up above someplace. You don't forget these things easily. They create resentment in you. You are being discriminated against and segregated and you wonder why. You build, over and above the resentment, a sense of rebellion against being pushed around to one side, labeled with a racial tag. You resolve that you are only going to take as much of this kind of thing as you just have to. What you have to take today, you are going to fight against tomorrow.

Maybe it was a good thing for me that I met Old Man Jim Crow during the tender years, for in later years I would learn that I hadn't yet seen the worst. To me "Jim Crow" was always symbolized by a mean, miserable old man who had lost the power to think or feel for others; and so we referred to racial segregation as Old Man Jim Crow.

In addition to finding out later in life that Old Man Jim Crow was even more wicked than I imagined as a boy, I would also learn that there are a lot of people who are not blacks who dislike injustice and are willing to help do something to defeat it.

2

From the "Pepper Street Gang" to UCLA

SOMETIMES IT SEEMS my teen-age days in Pasadena were like a game of tug of war. There were good influences working toward making me a positive, worthwhile person and bad influences that could have dragged me down even before I got to college.

Youngsters in those days, just as today, seemed to feel it was pretty corny when older folks said that home, school, and church are most important in shaping the lives of young people. Corny or not, I can look back and see how my family, my teachers, my coaches, and my feeling toward our family church all combined to save me from making a mess of my life.

We had certain disadvantages as a family—disadvantages which I've mentioned before. Often when a family is in substandard financial condition, youngsters use this as an excuse to steal or do other immoral things to get the luxuries they want for themselves—or even to try to help the whole family. Some parents, unfortunately, will make things worse, either by failing to supervise youngsters properly or by accepting what is brought home without asking where it came from.

My brothers and I knew we would never be able to get away with that kind of thing as long as my mother was around. She didn't preach at us very much about being decent kids. She didn't talk a lot, but she knew how to make decisions whenever crises arose. Most important of all, she set an example by the way she showed her independence of others and struggled and sacrificed so unselfishly for us. This gave us a sense of obligation not only to help her and to make things easier for her, but to do it in a way she could proudly accept.

I never had better moments as a boy than when I could see my mother turn the corner into our street, dragging wearily home from her domestic work, and I could run to greet her by giving her a dollar I had earned for mowing someone's lawn or collecting junk or selling newspapers or hawking hot dogs at sports events in the Pasadena Rose Bowl.

Don't get me wrong. I was no goody-goody. I

came pretty close to falling a victim to the circumstances under which we were living—circumstances with which a lot of kids are familiar. You come home from school. There's nobody there, nothing in the house to eat. You have time on your hands. There was one period in my boyhood days—a brief one, thank goodness—when I got myself into the category known as juvenile delinquent.

I joined a gang. We didn't go around mugging people or having deadly street fights or snatching pocketbooks, but we did get into a lot of mischief and trouble with the police.

We called ourselves the "Pepper Street Gang." We hid out on the local golf course and when a long drive produced a flying golf ball, it automatically became our property, only to be resold (when we had collected a quantity) to the golfers back at the club. This operation not only brought us profits but lots of hilarity as the poor golfers wondered what had happened to their balls and possibly later repurchased one they had lost to us.

We did the same thing with baseballs that were hit out of the park.

We threw dirt and old fruit at passing cars and stole fresh fruit from stands. We did all the mischievous things we could think of and our greatest thrill came from out-running the police when they arrived on the scene, summoned by some outraged citizen.

We were a kind of United Nations gang—black, Japanese, Mexican, and white. Once we swam delightedly in the city water reservoir and got hauled off to the police station.

We never did get into any really serious trouble with the law, but there's always a thin line between mischief and malice.

One of my teachers who took a great interest in me impressed me with the suggestion that I should leave the gang, not only for my mother's sake, but for my own.

"Jack," he told me, "you know in your own heart that you don't belong in a gang—at least, not with a crowd that might steer you into trouble. Most of you youngsters who fall into the gang habit do so because you're afraid to be considered different, afraid not to follow the crowd. Well, let me tell you something. Only first-class suckers allow others to lead them into doing what they don't want to do. It takes guts and imagination and intelligence to go your own way, to be different—to stand up on your own two feet. You'll not only be a much better kid, but much better off, too, if you resist doing wrong and don't worry about being called 'chicken.' "

Maybe that teacher thought I wasn't paying any attention to him. Well, nothing could have been further from the truth. Even if I didn't admit it openly, he was right. Furthermore, I started to apply his advice, and I've continued to live by this philosophy ever since.

It was such thinking that made it possible for me to resist the temptations of drinking and smoking, which come early in the life of a teenager. I didn't pass up these so-called pleasures because I was a model of morality. I think my main reasons for staying away from alcohol and tobacco were that I didn't want to do things to follow the crowd and I did want to be a good athlete with a strong constitution and powers of endurance.

So many of our splendid sportsmen break all the rules and think they are getting away with something because no ill effects show up immediately. They continue to win and they believe that their bodies are immune to deterioration. Down the line somewhere—and I've seen it happen so many times—the competition gets awfully rough. They need that one extra ounce of energy, that one little decisive pull which makes the difference between victory and defeat. They find they don't have the reserves. It is honorable to lose when you have given your best and when you have taken every precaution to stay in top condition. On the other hand, you feel terrible when you realize that it wasn't the opposition that defeated you but you who defeated yourself.

I'm certain that my determination to remain physically shipshape paid off for me in the success I began to enjoy in high school and junior college.

Ever since I had given all the enthusiasm of an eight-year-old to playing with a rag ball and stick in front of our home in Pasadena, I had become increasingly interested in all forms of sports. At John Muir Technical High I earned letters in football, basketball, baseball, and track. I had an innate, fierce sense of competition, and as early as those high school days I got the reputation of being very aggressive. My coaches liked this—but the opposition coaches and players didn't.

As a result, I found many times that competing teams seemed to concentrate on trying to stop me, to show me up, to bait me with taunts and nasty remarks instead of fighting the team I was on. Most of the time when I discovered I was being made the main target—or that my opponents were trying to make me lose my temper—it just made me all the more determined to win.

My brother Frank believed I could win any sports contest anywhere, at any time, and under any conditions. Frank's confidence and his constant advice made me feel very good. I tried hard to justify it. Frank swore up and down that it was unfair, as my high school days drew to a close, that I had not been scouted by a big college and offered an athletic scholarship. When I decided to attend Pasadena Junior College, Frank helped me prepare to go out for the Pasadena football team.

In those early days at Pasadena it looked as though luck was against me. I broke my ankle in one of the first practice sessions and was forced to sit on the bench. After my ankle healed in mid-season, I played first-string quarterback. We won five out of the remaining six games. The sixth game ended in a scoreless tie.

I began getting the kind of attention from the sports writers and scouts that Frank thought I should have received all along. The sports writers praised my football and basketball performances and gave me a lot of credit for my work with the track and baseball teams.

I got one of my deepest thrills in the spring of 1938 when I participated in a conference track meet and a championship ball game, both in the same day and in two different cities. I had a great urge to run in the meet, and yet I felt I couldn't miss the baseball game. In what turned out to be

At UCLA, Robinson won the national collegiate championship in the long jump (top), led the basketball team in scoring for two straight seasons (right), earned All-American honors in football, and played shortstop on the baseball team.

one of the fastest-moving days of my life, I went to Pomona in the early afternoon to take part in the broad jumps and later drove to Glendale to make the ball game.

I set a new running broad jump record at the track meet that day—25 feet 6 1/2 inches. Playing shortstop with the Pasadena team later in the afternoon, I was credited with helping our team win the championship. I could look back at a season in which my batting average was .417 with twenty-five stolen bases in twenty-four games. This earned me the title of the most valuable junior college player in Southern California.

Much as I loved baseball, it was my football playing at Pasadena that started getting me a lot of attention. In the fall of 1938 our team became the junior college champions with eleven straight wins. I had a score of 131 points and tallied more than one thousand yards from scrimmage.

The following year I enrolled at the University of California in Los Angeles. I selected UCLA— where I had to pay a token tuition—in spite of the fact that finally the offers of scholarships which I had hoped for on graduating from high school began to come my way. Some of the offers were mighty attractive. One major school offered to take care of my tuition and spending money and to arrange for a scholarship for any girl of my choice, as well as for a free apartment that would be for my mother.

Some of my closest buddies thought I was touched in the head when I turned down this offer and others. There was one main reason: I didn't have the heart to go to a school so far from home that my brother Frank wouldn't be able to see the games in which I participated.

Ironically, before any of those games were played, Frank was injured in a motorcycle accident and died a few hours later.

It took me a long time to recover from the loss of my brother. It might have been the necessity for getting my mind fixed on something other than his tragic death that spurred me on toward a football career at UCLA, which put me into the national spotlight.

The university had a great team. I had great admiration for the other black halfback, Kenny Washington, whom I consider the greatest football player I have ever known. That first season our team racked up victories in six games and tied four. I got a chance to work out as a trackster on the football team, averaging twelve yards per carry and twenty-one yards per punt return. There were some major thrills in a game against

Stanford; thrills which included a sixty-five-yard run. Then there was an eighty-two-yard run which sewed up the game with Oregon.

Our team didn't live up to its reputation that year after all, but in spite of this disappointment, the excitement of the games, those triumphs, had made me feel wonderful. In 1940 and 1941 I was high-scorer in the Southern Division of the Pacific Coast Conference and was named to the all-division team. Broad-jumping also was claiming my time. During my two years at UCLA I managed to become the first person in the school's history to win major letters in four different sports.

Of all the sports in which I was active, baseball had seemed the least important. In amateur ball I had a .400 average in the state tournament. I didn't do that well at UCLA. I played shortstop and found sheer delight in running bases.

There was a dark shadow growing larger, over all the fun and glory in my sports success. After I had been at UCLA for two years, the shadow became something I could no longer ignore.

I was earning recognition. Things were happening for me which I knew would have made my dead brother Frank proud. Yet I could not feel happy. The old Robinson family enemy—lack of money—was plaguing us again.

My mother was still going about her dreary work routine. Our Uncle Burton was aging and ill. My brother Edgar and sister, Willa Mae, both had families of their own to support. Mack was home and working, but the help he could give wasn't adequate.

I began to feel more and more that I was being selfish in trying to stick it out in college. There was little tuition to pay at UCLA, but there were all the usual expenses. I picked up odd jobs here and there, hawking candy and hot dogs at the Rose Bowl, working as a bus boy in a restaurant and a part-time janitor at the college.

Despite all this, I was unable to help my mother the way I thought I should. Then Mack married and that meant less money coming into the home. I had loved practically every minute of my college days, but now they had to end. I decided I'd have to leave school and get a full-time job.

Both Mack and my mother were horrified. They tried to talk me into sticking it out. The one factor that gave me more stubborn determination than anything else was my mother's unselfish attitude.

"I can get along fine without your money," she pleaded. "I did it when you boys couldn't wipe your noses and I can still do it."

That settled things for me. Perhaps she could be that generous—even though the years of struggling were visibly showing—but I couldn't accept that much generosity.

I don't want to make it sound as though I was being heroic for my mother's sake alone; there was another consideration. At UCLA I had met and begun to feel close to a very sweet girl.

3

Rachel Isum

WHEN I FIRST MET RACHEL ISUM, I recognized immediately that she was a pretty girl; but I had no idea she would become the most important girl in my life.

Ray Bartlett, my best friend at UCLA, was responsible for our meeting. One afternoon when I was engaged in some of the part-time work I did around the school, Ray came into the student lounge with two girls. I knew one of them.

"This is Rachel Isum, Jackie Robinson," Ray said, introducing me to her.

We exchanged the niceties people trade when introduced. I was feeling a little out of place. What with school work, sports, and home responsibilities, I hadn't much time for socializing on campus. It was impossible not to feel at ease with Rae, however. She had an awfully nice smile and a kind of mysterious mischief in her eyes. Soon she and I were talking comfortably.

I walked with her to the parking lot and it was just one of those things. I think we both felt we were going to see each other again. We did. There was one problem.

I am the kind of person who is easily misunderstood—and what is more, sometimes I don't care. By this I mean that as long as I am being sincere and honest with myself, why worry about the opinions of others? I was concerned however about Rae's opinion. At first, she misunderstood one thing about me. She had seen me play at Pasadena Junior College and gotten the impression that I was cocky because of the way I stood at backfield with my hands on my hips.

So at this first meeting Rae didn't exactly rate me as one of her favorite people.

She had every reason, on the surface, to think I was cocky. Actually I wasn't and never have been. I simply hate hypocrisy, and when you become an athlete on campus, you frequently come into contact with insincere people. Some girls like you not for yourself but because you are supposed to be a celebrity. When you hit a slump, they will wander off to the next guy who is riding the popularity wave.

It wasn't long after I met Rae that I realized she was not the type to care for a person just because he was popular with others. I liked that in her. It broke down my determination not to "go steady" with anyone on campus. On our first date we went to the Homecoming Game and dance at the Biltmore in Los Angeles.

After that dance, we saw a great deal of each other.

I knew that Rae was the girl for me because of her sincere and outspoken interest in my career and her concern for me as a person. She wasn't the type to moon up to a guy and agree with everything he said and tell him how great he was. She couldn't be a hypocrite. If she liked you, she liked you all the way; she felt she had the right and duty to be honest about your shortcomings as well as your good points.

It didn't take Rae long to see that I was quick to react to anything I considered unjust. As I have said before, I wasn't given to looking for trouble, but I was quick to sense an injustice or a slur, and when trouble came looking for me, I never backed off.

This disposition had its roots, I think, in my boyhood days in Pasadena when I became aware that there were some people who tried to walk over you because of your color; some who wanted to deny you an equal chance or even a meal or a seat you wanted to buy in the orchestra of a two-by-four neighborhood movie house. It went back to my resolve that, whatever the consequences, I was never going to be anybody's doormat.

Rae knew how I felt about these things. During my sports career at Muir High, Pasadena Junior College, and UCLA I had earned a reputation in the eyes of some as "a guy who won't take any stuff." Others thought of me as a "trouble-maker."

In those days, in school sports, the black athlete in California was just beginning to be accepted in integrated situations. He wasn't really accepted, because coaches and universities were looking for only those blacks who would be docile. If a white called you a nasty name during a game, you weren't supposed to answer back. If you were deliberately fouled or spiked, you weren't expected to protest in the natural way whites would.

I never accepted this method of "getting ahead." I'm certain that the fact that I always took up for myself, reacted with indignation, and was ready to accept any challenge caused certain schools to withhold scholarship offers from me before I started getting a great deal of national publicity.

I don't mean to say that I was right every time I blew my top or lost my temper, or that I was wise in not controlling myself. There is such a thing—

and I was to learn this later—as being smart and taking an injustice without being a coward.

This was what Rae began to teach me. I'm sure I'd heard such advice before but not from anyone who had the power to calm me down and cool me off as she could.

I had been shy and withdrawn with all the girls I had known before. But I could talk to Rae. I could express whatever was in my heart and sometimes exhaust my temper and my frustration in the process. She knew how to listen, how to understand, how to say exactly the right thing to make me feel better or to make me realize I was barking up the wrong tree.

The day I made my decision to leave school, I was sure Rae would object violently. She was preparing herself to become a nurse and she was impressed with the importance of education, especially for people of our race. I had all the confidence in the world in Rae's judgment. Even so, the really big decisions you make in life, you have to make on your own. No one, no matter how beloved or how close to you, can do this for you. I knew that quitting school was right for me no matter what arguments Rae advanced.

I prepared myself to answer all the things she might say. You can imagine how relieved and surprised I was when, after listening carefully to all my reasoning, Rae didn't have a word of opposition to my plans.

Immediate in my planning was acceptance of a job as assistant athletic director at a youngsters' work camp in northern California. I would be drawing a Government paycheck from the National Youth Administration. I would be in charge of sports activities, games, and calisthenics, supervising kids who had grown up under substandard conditions.

I looked forward eagerly to the challenge of the new job. Not only would it enable me to help out at home, but maybe I could do some good for those kids.

Within a few weeks I reported for duty. From the beginning I found myself intensely involved with the youngsters, not just as an instructor but as a friend. I learned that no matter what their background, no matter how much trouble they had been involved in, these youngsters were starved for attention, understanding, and intelligent discipline. I could have kept the job for a long time in terms of the satisfaction it gave me. But the war came along and caused the closing of the Youth Administration Camps. At about that time I began to play pro football.

In those days discrimination existed in professional football just as it did in professional baseball. The major teams were not looking for black players. I joined the Honolulu Bears and, after that, went on a twelve-game tour with the Los Angeles Bulldogs. The pay was excellent, but there are brief seasons in this work. After it was over, I had a job—not a particularly challenging one—working with a construction company near Pearl Harbor.

I was on a ship coming home from Hawaii that fateful December day when the Japanese loosed the bombs which drew America into World War II. I guess I should have realized right then that it wouldn't be long before I'd be getting my ''greetings'' from Uncle Sam.

4

OCS and the K.C. Monarchs

SOME OF MY FRIENDS thought I shouldn't even be considering the possibility of being drafted into the armed forces. Even if I were called, they pointed out, I had two good "outs." My mother depended mainly on me for support and I had a bum ankle which I'd acquired in the old football days. Frequently the bone chips in the ankle would begin to move, inflaming the joint, swelling, and giving me great pain.

I had no intention of trying to use these two excuses—legitimate as they might have been—to avoid serving my country. In addition to the fact that I was aware of my patriotic duty, I wasn't going to give any of the sports writers the chance to say that I was big and bad on the baseball and football fields and a slacker when it came to military service. I felt quite relieved when I passed the physical, even though I was placed on "limited service."

From a reception center in California I shipped out to a cavalry outfit at Fort Riley, Kansas, for basic training. I applied for Officers Candidate School and got my second lieutenant's bars in 1943, drawing an assignment to the 761st Tank Battalion of the Second Armored Division at Camp Hood, Texas.

Getting to be an officer in the United States Army didn't happen as easily as it sounds. When I first applied for OCS I was amazed to learn that Fort Riley did not accept blacks as officer candidates. It was a lucky thing for us that Joe Louis, who was in the Army then, came to Fort Riley. I told the world heavyweight champion how things operated at the post. No one ever admitted officially that you couldn't become an officer if you were a black. They just never qualified any black who applied. Joe Louis doesn't talk much but he certainly knows how to act. He got in touch with some influential friends in Washington, who saw to it that an investigation was started. It wasn't long before the authorities at Fort Riley discovered that a few black applicants, including me, were qualified after all.

I was inspired by what Louis had done. I think

the example he set in coming to our aid helped me make up my own mind to try to do something to help the black enlisted men around me who were living under intolerable conditions.

Ironically, I had been assigned as a special service and morale officer for a black company. I say it was ironic because you could have put the morale of those fellows into a small thimble. Right on the post, for instance, men who were being prepared to fight and die for democracy on foreign soil were forced to stand on long lines just to get a seat in the post exchange. The reason? It wasn't first come, first served in that Army PX. There were certain seats—a very small number—set aside for black soldiers. This was only one instance of the unjust way black troops were being humiliated and jim-crowed.

All about me, in hushed but bitter voices, I heard black soldiers giving voice to the obvious question. Why were they being asked to fight for the very democracy which they were denied even while serving in the uniform of their country?

When some of the men came to me and protested I decided to see what I could do to bring about some changes.

I telephoned the provost marshal and stated my objections to the conditions in the post exchange. When I informed him that the morale of

Overcoming racial discrimination in the army as well as in civilian life, Robinson became a second lieutenant in January 1943. He served in the military for two years.

the black troops was very low, he replied that if all soldiers were given the same facilities, it would hurt the morale of the whites. We got into a hot argument. I forgot that I was talking to a superior officer, a major, and let him know exactly what I thought of him.

The provost marshal wouldn't budge an inch. I appealed to the commanding officer of the battalion, Colonel Longley. He told me that he didn't approve of discrimination and promised that he would write higher authorities to seek a reversal of the policy.

The colonel kept his promise and registered a strong and powerful protest. It wasn't long before things started changing at Fort Riley. Soon after this I was transferred to Camp Hood, Texas to take over the platoon of the 761st battalion.

I knew just as much about running a tank unit as I did about making blintzes. If it hadn't been for the wonderful cooperation the noncoms and the other enlisted men in the unit gave me, the job of getting that group ready to go overseas would have been one of the most outstanding failures of World War II. I got their help because I put it on the line with the men right at the beginning. I told them I had no experience in the job to which I had been assigned. By leveling with them and not trying to bluff my way through, I was able to spark terrific team spirit. As a matter of fact, our platoon received special commendation.

Because of the work the unit had done, I received an unusual offer. It was fairly well understood that my limited service status would prevent me from going overseas. However, my superiors wanted to keep me in command of the group which had done such a splendid job in training. I was asked if I would accept overseas duty. It wasn't an order. In fact, if I agreed, I would have to sign a document relieving the Army of any responsibility in the event I was injured. I gave the idea some serious thought because, after all, it meant that I would be giving up some of the most important benefits a soldier has when he goes into combat duty. Finally I decided to accept.

It wasn't going to be that simple, I learned. The medics decided to hospitalize me and X-ray the ankle very carefully before granting me permission to go overseas. I was sent to a hospital thirty miles away from camp and it was while I was there that I had a very serious conflict.

One evening I got leave from the hospital authorities to visit the post. The friends I intended to see at camp were away on leave, so I decided to take the bus back to the hospital. As I was leaving the post officers' club the wife of one of my friends and fellow officers asked if she could go with me. She would be taking the same bus home. It was late and she wanted some company.

The girl was good-looking and very fair-skinned. She might easily have been mistaken for a white person.

We rode along in the bus, talking. I was unaware that we were being stared at by some of the passengers. As I was in the middle of a sentence, I was puzzled to see a look of fear come across the girl's face. I realized suddenly that the bus had stopped. The driver, glaring at me, was shouting a command for me to leave my seat and get to the back of the bus.

I was so astounded at first that I couldn't even speak. We were still on the Army post and there were orders that there was to be no segregation in transportation there.

The driver jumped up from his seat, strode down the aisle, and stood over me menacingly.

"Get to the back of the bus where colored people belong," he ordered. "Come on. Move, or there'll be trouble."

The girl sitting next to me started to get up. I pulled her back down in the seat and tried to get a grip on the anger which was rising inside of me.

"Look, buddy," I told the driver. "You'd better just drive this bus and leave me alone. I'm not moving anywhere."

A tense silence had fallen over the bus. The driver stared at me for a minute. Then he turned angrily and went back to his seat.

"You just better not be sitting in that seat when we get to the gate," he shouted back as he started the motor again. "If you are, there's going to be trouble."

I was choked up with rage and sick of hearing this prejudiced man talk about "trouble."

"Make all the trouble you want," I called back to him. "I'm not moving."

At the gate the driver jumped off the bus before anyone else. As my friend and I got off, the driver pointed me out to a dispatcher.

"This nigger's been giving me a hard time," he accused.

The ugly word made me shake with indignation. I was trying very hard not to lose my control. I exchanged a few hot words with the driver and walked off with the girl.

I had only gone a few steps when two military policemen walked up. The bus company had lodged a complaint with the provost marshal. I was politely asked to get into a jeep and go to his office. I hated to leave the girl to continue her trip alone but there was no alternative.

The provost marshal, a captain, made it quite obvious from the beginning that he believed the proper place for blacks was at the back of the buses. He called me "uppity," asked if I were trying to start a race riot, and finally dismissed me with the accusation that I was a troublemaker. Charges would be filed against me, he threatened.

When I returned to the hospital that night, word of the incident had already arrived there. It was lucky for me because a friendly officer confided that he had received a report that a "drunken Negro officer" had attempted to start a fight on a bus. If it hadn't been for this officer, I would never have known I was to be charged with being drunk. Since I'd never had a drink in my life, I quickly agreed to undergo a test right on the spot to disprove the "drunk" charge. The test showed negative results, of course.

In addition to being accused of drunkenness, when the charges were filed, I discovered I had been accused of "conduct unbecoming an officer, willful disobedience of an order, and disrespect to a commanding officer."

Some of my fellow black officers got together to help me fight the unjust charges. They wrote letters to the Pittsburgh *Courier* and Chicago *Defender*, two outstanding national black weeklies. Only the *Courier* responded. Publicity which appeared in that newspaper resulted in wires and letters being sent to the War Department by concerned citizens. In the end, the bus charges were eliminated and I was to face charges only relating to the incident in the captain's quarters. Investigation later proved how baseless these accusations were and all charges were dropped. However, before this happened, because of the impending court-martial, I was transferred to another unit and did not get a chance to go overseas with my organization. Shortly after charges were dropped, I was honorably discharged.

Truthfully, I would have preferred the danger of overseas duty to the kind of life a black soldier lived in a Southern training camp and in nearby cities. You went to town and there was one USO for blacks and another for whites. There were certain streets you weren't even allowed to walk on. White streets, I guess you'd call them. In the main, the kind of girls I saw keeping company with our soldiers were girls who didn't interest me. Besides, I had a one-track mind which was concentrated on the girl I loved—Rae.

If you ever want to test your affection for your girl, just get yourself drafted into service. I missed Rae desperately. The only relief I could get was through writing her and receiving her letters. We corresponded almost daily. Hearing from Rae was my salvation. For a few months we were writing about how we felt toward each other, how much we missed each other. We wrote about all the great things we were going to do together after the war. It was a happy exchange. But soon, to an increasingly critical degree, dissension began to appear in our letters.

Rae was studying nursing in San Francisco. She became restless and wanted to do something more than sit around waiting, hoping I'd be able to make it back home. She had a brother who was missing in the European theater and this increased her fears about what could happen to me. Finally, completely bored with the home front and wanting to get her mind off her worries, she decided she would join the WAC. Believing her brother to be dead, she had convinced herself that it was her duty to enlist.

I didn't want Rae to go into the service. We argued about it in our letters. One night I was feeling so strongly about her insistence on joining up that I wrote an impatient letter and told her if she had to have her way about our difference in this matter, I could see no point in our remaining engaged. Rae didn't answer by letter. She mailed me a small box which contained the engagement ring I had given her.

I was certain that I had lost Rae for good. I didn't want to lose her, but I had too much pride to admit it. I had no way of knowing that she was feeling the same way.

I told myself defiantly that Rae wasn't the only girl on earth. I tried not to think about the fact that I really thought of her as the only girl for me. I even began dating another girl who lived close to the Army post.

Trying to turn to someone else just wasn't any good. Finally I simply gave up trying to forget Rae and settled down into a long period of misery and regret over my reckless, impulsive anger. Frankly I didn't see how I could reshape the dreams of the four years during which Rae and I had known each other.

Several months after our breakup, en route to another assignment, I got a chance to visit my home in Pasadena. I was thrilled at the thought of seeing my family, but sad because I would be so close to Rae and unable to see her. By this time I was certain our love was a lost cause. Seeing each other would probably only make both of us miserable. I was miserable anyhow during that visit home. My mother noticed it and didn't say anything for a few days. Then she couldn't stand it any longer.

''Jackie,'' she said to me abruptly one day, ''you know you want to call Rachel.''

I couldn't deny that—not even to myself.

I put through the phone call and after the first few words with Rae I set some sort of record getting from Pasadena to San Francisco. Making up was almost as sweet as falling in love the first time. However, I think we both learned a lesson— never again to allow misunderstanding to make us forget our deep mutual love.

You can bet I was in love. I wanted to stay in San Francisco for the rest of my leave so I could be close to the girl I had won back. The state of my pocketbook made a hotel out of the question. So I slept in my ancient jalopy every night and fretted through the days until Rae had finished work. Her brother had been found, and she no longer felt that she had an obligation to join the WAC.

The leave was up all too soon. I had to report back to duty. I had the satisfaction of knowing, however, that even though Rae hadn't taken the ring back, she was still my girl.

Now that we had weathered a critical storm, I was more than ever anxious for the day to come when my girl would become Mrs. Jackie Robinson. The thought thrilled and depressed me. I was thrilled because I visualized a life of perfect happiness with Rae as my wife. I was depressed because getting married would mean I'd really have to make an excellent salary. After all, there was still my mother to consider.

It was a happy coincidence that just at this period, when I was casting about in my mind to settle on an approach to a postwar job or career, I ran into a fellow GI who began telling me what big opportunities there were in professional Negro baseball. He himself had pitched for the Kansas City Monarchs in the Negro American League. The team was on the lookout for good players, he told me. Why didn't I write and ask about a job?

I acted on this advice promptly, for I had been informed that I was to receive a medical discharge from the Army.

The discharge came through in November, 1944. I accepted a job as a basketball coach of a small black college in Austin, Texas. The work was challenging. The team I was handling developed very well. But by now my job with the Kansas City Monarchs had come through. This was it, I decided. I accepted and took off for spring training with the team in Houston.

It was April of 1945 and I was a professional.

My Army friend had told me the pay was pretty good in Negro pro baseball. He had told the truth. He had told me it was a great life, being a baseball pro. That wasn't so true. Not for me, anyhow.

In the first place, the travel schedules were hectic.

We played in Kansas City, covered the entire Middle West, and had some games in the South and East. On one typical occasion we left Kansas City by bus on a Sunday night, reached Philadelphia late Tuesday afternoon, and hit the ball park that night. The next day we were off again.

This frantic hopping back and forth across the country might have been more bearable if we could have counted on some decent meals. They were few and far between. Many of the places in which we stayed had no hotels. Some black hotels were simply makeshift places to sleep with no dining rooms. Getting into white hotels in the South and some other sections of the country was out of the question. Often we were refused service even at roadside places. There were some places where we could not be served a hot meal but were allowed to carry out hamburgers and coffee in a paper bag. We had to eat outside or on the bus. I'd be rich if I had a dollar for every time I settled for a cardboard plate of cold cuts after a long and tiring trip. It was all pretty depressing.

I would have been a lot more enthusiastic, in spite of these problems, if I could have believed there was a future for the black player in the major leagues. I knew that people all over the country— the black press and liberal white sports writers— were pounding away at the doors which barred blacks from the majors. That didn't mean much to me because I didn't believe anything would

Robinson broke into professional baseball in 1945 with the Kansas City Monarchs of the old Negro Leagues. Barred from major league teams, other talented black players toiled in obscurity in the Negro Leagues for their entire careers.

happen to change the picture during my baseball career. I thought the breakthrough would take a long, long time.

We black players weren't bitter about the situation. Yet many of us felt that it was unrealistic to invest our lives in a sport where progress was limited by discrimination.

To aggravate the whole situation, I began to sense that I might lose Rae. Although she had been most understanding about my accepting the job as a college coach in Texas, then going off with the Monarchs, I knew she was disappointed. She had hoped I would settle down in California after coming out of the service. We hardly saw each other because of the breakneck schedule of the team.

To sum it all up, I was beginning to feel less and less happy about being in Negro baseball. But where could I go? What could I do that would place me in a position to continue to help my mother and to marry Rae?

I didn't know the answer. A few thousand miles away from Texas a distinguished-looking, white-haired, and courageous man, whom I had never met, did.

His name was Branch Rickey, the boss of the Brooklyn Dodgers.

5

Enter Branch Rickey

To ME BRANCH RICKEY was only the name of a man identified with the ruling class—the club owners of American baseball. If I'd ever had any thoughts about Mr. Rickey, they could only have been to identify him as a member of that small band of influential men who were content to control what everyone called America's favorite sport and who denied black players a chance to get into it. If I had known anything about Mr. Rickey's background, his convictions, and his plans for the future, I wouldn't have been so downhearted and so cynical about the future for a black in the major leagues.

But I didn't know.

I didn't know that in spite of the fact that he had grown up in southern Ohio, close to the Kentucky line, Branch Rickey even as a boy had inwardly rejected the not-too-liberal racial atmosphere of his community. There was a deep religious sense in the Rickey household, stemming from the boy's parents. They were the kind of devout people who were unable to talk about the Fatherhood of God without acknowledging the brotherhood of man.

Even with his upbringing, Branch Rickey might not have written history into modern baseball if it hadn't been for an incident which had burned into his consciousness an awareness of the terrible effects of race prejudice.

Back in 1910 Mr. Rickey was a coach for Ohio Wesleyan. The team traveled to South Bend, Indiana. Coach Rickey and a few of the other men registered at a hotel and went to their rooms, leaving the rest of the players at the desk to sign in. One of the men, as yet unregistered, was Charley Thomas, a black.

A few minutes later Mr. Rickey was summoned downstairs to the manager's office. The hotel man, pointing at Thomas, came brutally to the point.

"We don't register niggers in this hotel," he told Mr. Rickey.

The young coach thought swiftly. Gently he moved the humiliated black player out of range of the manager's insults. "You sit down a couple of minutes. We'll see what we can do," Branch Rickey told him.

Back at the manager's desk, Mr. Rickey, suppressing his indignation, begged the manager to be allowed to share his own suite with Thomas. The manager refused to give in until coach Rickey took a long shot. He threatened to move the whole team to another hotel. Branch Rickey knew quite well this was an empty threat, for none of the suitable hotels in the city accepted black guests.

Seeing the manager's hesitation, Mr. Rickey pushed his advantage. "Just give me a cot for him to sleep on in my room?" he asked.

The manager gave in reluctantly.

Charley Thomas had a place to sleep that night. But he couldn't sleep.

"He sat on that cot," Branch Rickey told friends years later, "silent for a while. Then tears he couldn't hold back came into his eyes and his whole body shook with emotion. I sat watching him, not knowing what to do until he began tearing at one hand with the other—just as if he were trying to scratch the skin off his hands with his finger nails."

"Charley," the coach cried out. "What are you doing?"

"It's my hands," Charley Thomas sobbed. "They're black. If only they were white. I'd be as good as anybody then, wouldn't I Mr. Rickey, if only they were white?"

The tears in the eys of Charley Thomas were matched by tears that rose to the eyes of Branch Rickey. The coach spoke with gentle determination.

"The day will come, Charley, when they won't have to be white."

The resolve which was born in the heart of a white coach that night could not ease the heartache of a rejected black player. Charley Thomas wept all night long.

Branch Rickey never forgot those sobs of a boy who had wanted to skin himself of his blackness in order to be accepted.

Throughout thirty years as player, manager, and front office executive, Branch Rickey had nursed a growing anger against the racial bigotry which kept the Charley Thomases out of hotel rooms and barred from the teams of major leagues. He had begun translating this anger into action as an executive in St. Louis. At that city's Sportsman's Park, now Busch Stadium, home field of the Browns and Cardinals, black fans had to sit in a Jim Crow section.

Quietly, behind the scenes, Mr. Rickey was

beginning his fight for equality. Often he had private talks with Sam Breadon, the owner of the Cardinals, trying to persuade him to take action to break the Jim Crow rule at the ball park. Breadon had the traditional reason for not seeing the point. He was afraid of losing the business of white people.

Just as I knew nothing of the inner struggle of Branch Rickey, very few people associated with him in the game knew how he felt. However, he commanded a great deal of respect as a shrewd businessman. For one thing, he was the author of the "farm" method by which clubs could build their playing strength and reserve on a really businesslike basis.

In 1943, thirty-three years after the Charley Thomas incident, Mr. Rickey succeeded Larry MacPhail as president of the Brooklyn Dodgers.

In this powerful position he became convinced that the opportunity was now at hand to bring baseball's walls of race prejudice crumbling down.

Soon after becoming boss of the Dodgers, Mr. Rickey made his first move. He called the club's board of directors together and announced that he wanted their permission to make the Brooklyn team the first to bring black players into the major leagues. Mr. Rickey was an eloquent and persuasive salesman. The directors agreed to his revolutionary proposal and also to allow him free rein.

Execution of his plan called for delicate handling on Mr. Rickey's part.

In the first place, he must be certain that news of his intentions did not get around.

In the second place, he had to be certain that when he launched the "noble experiment" he would be prepared to offer a player who had not only the talent but also the temperament to take the rough experience any front-runner confronts in surmounting a new hurdle.

The idea of a breakthrough for blacks in organized baseball did not originate with Mr. Rickey. Exclusion of blacks from America's national pastime was under a barrage of attack. Indeed, pressure had become so intense that in some Northern communities the issue had become a political one. In Boston a city councilman, Isadore Muchnick, who had a large group of black voters in his constituency, had threatened to press a bill banning Sunday baseball unless the Red Sox hired black players. While I was with the Monarchs, Wendell Smith, then sports editor of the Pittsburgh *Courier*, an influential black paper, arranged for two other players of the Negro league—Sam Jethroe of the Cleveland Buckeyes and Marvin Williams of the Philadelphia Stars—

and me to go to the tryout. The Boston club patted us on the back, said we had made a good showing, gave us application cards to fill out, and that was that. We honestly felt that they had simply gone through the motions of giving blacks a chance in order to avoid further criticism.

Boston was not the only place where the pressure was being applied. In many cities respected sports writers, organizations, and public officials were echoing the argument that if a black is good enough to fight and die for his country, he certainly ought to be good enough to participate in American baseball.

The pressure was on in Brooklyn, too, in 1945. Branch Rickey was feeling it and there was no way he could defend himself by explaining his top-secret plan to break the barrier down. He could not reveal that he had a green light from his directors to take the bold step. He could not announce that he had launched a major scouting program which included surveying black players, evaluating them, checking their athletic and personal backgrounds. The scouts had moved not only to search out promising American blacks, but also to search for talent in Cuba, Mexico, Puerto Rico, Venezuela, and other countries where dark-skinned people live. Mr. Rickey had learned through his own "secret service" facilities that many American black players, back from the war, had gone into baseball in such countries and that they were doing a crackerjack job.

If other owners and players had learned of his plan, there could have been violent repercussions under the pressure of protest. Branch Rickey came up with a solution. His plan would quiet the hue and cry which was hounding him to integrate and it would, at the same time, allow him to accomplish his purpose in the cautious manner he preferred.

In the spring of 1945 Branch Rickey called a press conference and announced that he was forming a new Negro league. It was to be called the United States League. Anticipating the charge that he was side-stepping the issue of integration in baseball to create an all-black setup, Mr. Rickey predicted that his new team would be better organized than the existing Negro leagues and that its main purpose was to project a league which might eventually be absorbed into the majors.

Of course no one believed him. It was almost unanimously concluded that not only was Branch Rickey evading the issue but that he was greedy enough to want to extend the Dodger organization's business activities into Jim Crow baseball.

A storm of criticism broke over Mr. Rickey's

head. One of the people who felt Branch Rickey was insincere was Wendell Smith, the same editor who had taken three of us to Boston. Smith had a talk with Mr. Rickey. During the conversation the Dodger boss asked Smith whether any of us who had gone to Boston was really good enough for the majors.

"Jackie Robinson is," Smith answered.

During the next few months Mr. Rickey's scouts brought back reports. My name came up several more times. Finally my record and background were checked out.

Unhappy in the Negro league, wondering where to turn, thinking of giving up the game altogether so that I could keep my pride and my girl, Rae, I had no idea that in an office in downtown Brooklyn, Branch Rickey had made up his mind and decided my future. He had called in Clyde Sukeforth, one of his favorite scouts, and said, "Bring Jackie Robinson to talk to me."

It was August of 1945. My team, the Kansas City Monarchs, was in Chicago to play the Windy City's American Giants. It was one of those days when the only way to get relief from the heat is to make believe it doesn't exist. I was out on the field at Comiskey Park where the two teams were engaging in pregame practice.

"Robinson! Jackie Robinson."

The voice came from the railing near our dugout. I glanced in that direction and saw a white man beckoning to me. I walked over.

"You Jack Robinson?" he asked.

I admitted it.

"I'm Clyde Sukeforth," he said, holding out his hand. "I'm with the Brooklyn organization—the Dodgers. You know Mr. Rickey has a colored club now, the Brown Dodgers, and he's looking for top ballplayers. He's heard about you and he wanted me to watch you throw from the hole."

I grinned.

"Wrong time," I told the scout. "Couldn't be worse. You won't see me do any throwing from the hole tonight. I hurt my shoulder a couple of days ago and I'm not going to be playing for at least a week."

Sukeforth appeared to be disappointed.

"Anyhow," he said, "I'd like to talk to you after the game. I'm at the Stevens Hotel. How about meeting me there at the cigar stand in the lobby as soon as you can after the game is over?"

I hesitated. It was hard for me to believe anything worthwhile was going to happen. Bitter thoughts of the phony Boston tryout flashed across my mind. Yet Sukeforth looked like an earnest person. I had heard about the new Brown Dodgers Club, and what did I have to lose by wasting a few minutes talking? As long as I was realistic enough to realize it would probably be a waste, what was the harm?

"What did you say your name was?"

Sukeforth repeated it for me and we agreed to meet that night a little after eleven.

When we met, after exchanging formalities, the scout came right to the point. Mr. Rickey was interested in the possibility of my joining his Brown Dodgers. He wanted me to come to Brooklyn to talk to him about it. Since my injured shoulder would have me benched for a few days, Sukeforth pointed out, maybe this would be the best time to get a few days off to go to Brooklyn. The Dodgers would take care of my fare and expenses.

"Brooklyn?" I demanded. "Look, I can't just leave my team and run off to Brooklyn."

"But you're unable to play anyway. The Monarchs shouldn't mind," Sukeforth argued.

"Suppose they do? Suppose they fire me," I countered.

"I don't think they will," Sukeforth said gently. "Besides, I have a feeling that after you talk to Mr. Rickey the Monarchs will be unimportant to you."

I glanced at the scout, trying to figure out his meaning.

Wild fantasies crowded into my mind. What if

this was it? The big chance. Not just a job with another Negro club—the Brown Dodgers. What if the battle of Jericho in the majors was about to begin? What if the walls were about to come tumbling down?

"Whoa, fellow," I told myself. "You're getting carried away. Better rein up and get back to reality." I cared too much about getting that big chance to be exposing myself to ridiculous daydreams.

On the other hand, even if it was just another opportunity for another job in another Jim Crow club, why not find out what it was all about?

"What have I got to lose?" I said aloud.

"Nothing," murmured the Brooklyn scout. "Nothing! And plenty to gain."

Two hours later I was on a train racing toward Brooklyn and Branch Rickey.

It was a night which brought me no sleep. Below me, in his berth, Clyde Sukeforth was sleeping soundly. I was thinking. I was twenty-six years old and I had a dream, but I was afraid to take it out and examine it. Soon . . . soon I would know.

6

"Do You Have the Guts Not to Fight Back?"

BRANCH RICKEY had a luxuriously decorated office in the Brooklyn headquarters of the Dodger organization.

He had bushy brows, piercing eyes, a generous stomach, and the voice of a prophet, which could modulate from soft persuasion to thundering emphasis.

On the morning of August 28, 1945, when Clyde Sukeforth and I walked into Mr. Rickey's office, the baseball magnate rose from his leather swivel chair, puffing on his big cigar, and stuck out his hand in greeting.

He sat down, his eyes fixed on me as if he could see how I felt and knew what I was thinking.

"Do you drink?" he demanded.

"No, I don't," I answered.

He motioned me to a chair.

"You got a girl?" he asked.

The man's directness only increased the pounding tension I was trying so hard to conceal. I hadn't expected this question.

My answer was slow in coming but it was honest.

"I don't know," I said.

"What do you mean you don't know?"

"I mean that I *had* a girl, one to whom I'm engaged, but the way I've been traveling with the Monarchs, never seeing her or anything, a fellow can't be sure whether he's got a girl or not."

"Is she a fine girl, good family background, educated girl?"

"They don't come any finer, Mr. Rickey."

"Then you know doggone well you've got a girl. When we get through today you may want to call her up, because there are times when a man needs a woman by his side. By the way, are you under contract to the Monarchs?"

I answered that I was not; that I had a month-to-month, payday-to-payday agreement.

The Dodger boss relit his cigar, blew a smoke wreath, and leaned forward in his chair.

"Do you have any idea why I want to talk to you?" he demanded. "Do you really understand why you are here?"

"Well, Mr. Sukeforth said you wanted to talk to me about your new Brown Dodgers Club."

"That's what Mr. Sukeforth was supposed to tell you," Mr. Rickey said. "The truth is you are not here as a candidate for the Brooklyn Brown Dodgers. I've sent for you because I'm interested in you as a candidate for the Brooklyn National League Club. I think you can play in the major leagues. How do you feel about it?"

There it was! The realization of a dream I'd been pushing out of my mind because I simply couldn't believe it would ever come true.

How did I feel? It was hard to say. I didn't know how to put it into words or how to marshal my thoughts. I was dazzled, shocked, delighted, scared to death. I don't know whether I even answered the question. I know I answered the next question because it was specific—as specific as the pinch that wakes you out of a dream.

"You think you can play for Montreal?"

"Yes," I said.

Montreal! The Brooklyn Dodgers top farm club! This was the training school, the trial division to which Dodger hopefuls were taken, some of them failing, some emerging as full-fledged big-time major league stars.

Mr. Rickey considered my answer. Then he turned to Sukeforth.

"Think he can make the grade?" he asked the scout.

"He's good," Sukeforth answered. "He can run. He can field. He can hit."

With dramatic suddenness Mr. Rickey wheeled his swivel chair to face me. He pointed a finger challengingly.

"I know you are a good ballplayer," the Brooklyn boss said. "What I don't know is whether you have the guts."

"Guts," I repeated to myself wonderingly. I'd had a lot of things said about me, but no one had ever accused me of being a coward or running away from an issue—or even a fight.

What did Mr. Rickey mean? His voice was deep and rumbling as he told me.

"I'm going to tell you the truth, Jackie. I've investigated you thoroughly. They told me out in Pasadena that you're a racial agitator. They said at UCLA that in basketball you had trouble with coaches, players, and officials. I just want to tell you that my investigation convinced me that the criticisms are unjustified, that if you'd been white it would have been nothing. So I'm dismissing these rumors as not amounting to a hill of beans."

His rich voice deepened.

"The thing I want to convince you of is that we can't fight our way through this, Jackie. We've got no army. There's virtually nobody on our side. No owners, no umpires, very few newspapermen. And I'm afraid that many fans will be hostile. We'll be in a tough position, Jackie. We can win only if we can convince the world that I'm doing this because you're a great ballplayer and a fine gentleman.''

Mr. Rickey continued and it was almost as if he were talking to himself as well as to me. His sincerity charged the atmosphere in that office.

''So there's more than just playing,'' he said. ''I wish it meant only hits, runs and errors—only the things they put in the box score. Because you know—yes, you would know, Jackie—that a baseball box score is a democratic thing. It doesn't tell how big you are, what church you attend, what color you are, or how your father voted in the last election. It just tells what kind of baseball player you were on that particular day.''

''It's the box score that really counts—that and that alone—isn't it?'' I asked.

''It's all that *ought* to count! But it isn't! Maybe one of these days it *will* be all that counts. That's one of the reasons I've got you here, Jackie. If you're a good enough man, we can make this a start in the right direction. But let me tell you, it's going to take an awful lot of courage. Have you got the guts to play the game no matter what happens?''

He had left his desk and was leaning over in front of me, his face close to mine, his eyes measuring me.

"I think I can play the game, Mr. Rickey," I said. My nervousness was leaving me. I was filled with an excitement about what this man wanted to accomplish. It wasn't just making me the first in the majors. It wasn't just the buildup of one new star. We were standing at a closed door where many had knocked and none had been admitted. We were going to take hold of the knob, turn it, and walk in. But we had to walk carefully or it wouldn't work.

Mr. Rickey began to predict the kind of problems I would face; having vicious bean balls thrown at me; being attacked physically; being called dirty race-baiting names. He told me I'd have to permit all these things to happen to me and not lose my temper. I must never lose sight of our goal.

In those few minutes, experiences from most of my twenty-six years came to mind. Getting into fights as a kid because I was called "nigger," shouting back epithets when epithets were tossed at me in ball games, resenting insults and being willing to back up my resentment with my fists. I had always prided myself that I didn't start things but that I stood my ground when someone else did.

What was this white man asking of me now? Was he calling upon me to sell my manhood, my inbred militancy for some fame and money which might come to me?

"Mr. Rickey," I demanded suspiciously, "are you looking for a Negro who is afraid to fight back?"

The depth and passion of his voice and the classic simplicity of his reply thrilled me, shook me back into an understanding of what Branch Rickey was actually fighting for.

"I'm looking for a ballplayer, Jackie," he rumbled, "with guts enough *not* to fight back."

My interview with Branch Rickey lasted fully three hours. Once he had convinced me of the sincerity of his purpose and the logic of his approach, I was completely in tune with him. He proceeded to dramatize for me an animated rehearsal of some of the problems I would have to face. He did it so well that several times I had to make an effort to keep from getting angry, to make myself realize that he was acting a part and didn't mean some of the things he said.

"You're fielding a ground ball. A white player charges into you. He sneers at you, 'Next time get out of my way, you dirty black ____,'" Mr. Rickey said. "Can you walk away from him?

"He'll shout after you. He'll say all you niggers are yellow. He'll curse your parents. He'll say anything vile and low," Mr. Rickey said. "Can you turn your back on him?

"They'll taunt you, goad you. Anything to make you fight. Anything to bring about a race riot in the ball park. If they succeed, they'll be able to prove that having a Negro in baseball doesn't work. They'll be able to frighten people so they'll be afraid to come out to games.

"Suppose twelve hundred colored people, your own people, want to come on an excursion to see you. They're that proud of the first Negro in baseball. And suppose I say, No—no excursion. Will you understand why?"

I realized that he was saying that excessive enthusiasm on the part of blacks could be just as ruinous to the delicate experiment as the resentment of whites.

Rickey resumed his colorful descriptions of possible "incidents."

"You're at shortstop. I come down from first, stealing, flying in with my spikes high and I cut you in the leg. As the blood runs down your skin, I laugh in your face and say 'How do you like that, nigger boy?' What's your move?"

Branch Rickey did more than talk. He acted. He became a hostile umpire, not only calling unfair decisions but adding racial sneers to his injustice. He became a restaurant proprietor, telling me I couldn't eat with the rest of the team but that he would prepare sandwiches for me to take out. He became the hotel manager who had room for white ballplayers and the address of a flophouse where I could be accommodated—or the name of a private family willing to put me up.

A flurry of memories went through my mind as I heard and saw all of this. I had to reconstruct these memories before I could give an honest answer to myself and to Mr. Rickey, an answer to the unspoken question: Do you know how to turn the other cheek?

I remembered incidents which happened to me when I was a youngster in Pasadena. I remembered that even as a boy I had always reacted spiritedly when insulted or scorned. I had always fought back when attacked. I remembered getting into trouble in the service because I wouldn't take certain indignities offered to me or to my men. I remembered that down through the years the most vital basis of my personal creed had been that a man doesn't lie down to be walked over; he always stands up tall and ready to defend the most precious thing he owns—his manhood.

Yet Branch Rickey was asking me to take that creed and stow it away on some far back shelf of my mind.

I didn't know, sitting there in his office, how I

would be able to discipline myself, to control my rebellion at injustice. But I knew I would do it because I must. I had to learn to conquer and control myself because I sensed that the opportunity being offered me meant more than success for one Jackie Robinson. I had to do it because success would mean so much to the kids who would be coming up behind me. I wanted them to be able to feel that the color of their skins wouldn't hamper their dreams of making it in the majors. I had to do it because of my mother and the rest of my family and because of Rae, the girl I wanted to marry. Finally—to be perfectly honest—I had to do it for myself.

Maybe, someday, we would have kids of our own who would have it a little easier in life if one more barrier between people had been broken down. I had to do it because when a man like Branch Rickey invests faith in you, you want to be decent enough to strive to help the gamble pay off for him.

I will admit that following through on my decision to "turn the other cheek" was the most difficult task I faced during my baseball career. It wasn't easy to stifle my instinct to retaliate, strike back, protest. But I was constantly aware that if I could prove I could take it, I could also prove that a black could make it in the major leagues. That would be good, not only for my race, but also for the game of baseball and for the democratic image of America around the world.

When I walked out of Branch Rickey's office, I had an agreement to sign a contract with a $3,000 bonus and a $600-a-month salary to play ball with the Montreal Royals. I could tell only Rae and my mother. To the rest of the world it was to be a secret that a sincere white-haired man was about to offer the answer to a man who thirty-five years ago had cried in a hotel room all night long and torn at black hands he wished God had made white.

7

With the Montreal Royals

ON OCTOBER 23, on Mr. Rickey's instructions, I went to Montreal to meet with his son, Branch Rickey, Jr., and to sign my contract. The press was called in and the announcement made that I was now officially of the Brooklyn Dodger farm club, the Montreal Royals. It was the first time I had faced a large group of reporters. The newsmen were from Montreal and other Canadian cities, and they were extremely friendly. They fired questions at me with machine-gun rapidity. Most of the questions seemed irrelevant to me, but I was relieved that there didn't seem to be any hostility.

There was, naturally, a great deal of newspaper comment when the news broke that I was coming into organized ball.

"Jackie Robinson, the Negro signed by Brooklyn, will not make the grade in the big

History was made on October 23, 1945, when Jackie Robinson signed with the Montreal Royals, the top minor league team of the Brooklyn Dodgers. At left is Dodger president Branch Rickey, who persuaded Robinson to sign with the organization.

leagues next year or the next. . . ." wrote Jimmy Powers, sports editor of the New York *Daily News*. "Robinson is a thousand to one shot to make the grade."

The *Sporting News*, considered the Bible of baseball, declared: "He is . . . placed in competition with a vast number of younger, more skilled and more experienced players. This factor alone appears likely to beat him down."

Jack Horner, of North Carolina's Durham *Her-*

ald, stated: "The general impression in this city is that the Negro player will be so uncomfortable, embarrassed and out of place in organized baseball that he will soon get out, of his own accord."

But there were other writers who didn't share these opinions.

"Members of all races and from all sorts of places have been meeting together in the boxing ring on the may-the-best-man-win basis for so long that people with any sense at all have ceased to give it a second thought," wrote Bill Corum of the New York *Journal-American*. "It won't be many years until the same will be true of Negroes playing in organized baseball."

Dan Parker and Red Smith were among the large group of sports writers who went along with the idea of introducing democracy into the game.

Loyalty to the status quo was voiced by some baseball officials.

W. G. Bramham, the minor league commissioner, attacked Mr. Rickey: "Whenever I hear a white man, whether he be from the North, South, East or West, protesting what a friend he is to the Negro race, right then I know the Negro needs a bodyguard. It is those of the carpetbagger stripe of the white race who, under the guise of helping but in truth using the Negro for their own selfish interest, retard the race. . . . Father Divine will have to look to his laurels, for we can expect Rickey Temple to be in the course of construction in Harlem soon.''

Alvin Gardner, president of the Texas League, felt the same way. ''I'm positive you'll never see any Negro player on any of the teams in organized baseball in the South as long as the Jim Crow laws are in force,'' he declared.

Some of the white baseball owners and officials suddenly became very much concerned about the welfare of the Negro leagues. What would happen to the Negro clubs if the majors took away their talent, these owners and officials demanded.

Some were raising this question out of sincerity. Others brought it up as a possible stumbling block in the path of welcoming blacks into the majors.

There was even opposition—which died quickly—from the Kansas City club, challenging the right of the Dodger organization to take me away from them. They hastily withdrew this stumbling block when they realized that the black American public would not think kindly of them for helping to prevent the breakdown of race barriers in the game.

The third area of resistance was among the ballplayers themselves.

Dixie Walker, outfielder with the Dodgers,

looked at it this way: "As long as he's not with the Dodgers, I'm not worried."

Rogers Hornsby, a retired Texas ballplayer, thought Rickey was wrong. "It won't work," Hornsby said. "Ballplayers on the road live close together."

Bob Feller, the great pitcher, told reporters, "I can't foresee any future for Robinson in big league baseball. He is tied up in the shoulders and couldn't hit an inside pitch to save his neck. If he were a white man, I doubt if they would even consider him as big league material."

On the whole, however, most of the top people in the game, most of the sports writers, and the majority of the players adopted a wait-and-see attitude.

I wasn't upset or disturbed about those who were against the "noble experiment." I was more interested and keyed up about trying to prove to the "wait and see-ers" that a black could make the grade. I believed I could do it—especially since I was going to be able, at last, to marry the girl I loved.

"Marry her right away," Branch Rickey had suggested.

I didn't need anyone to push me to marry Rachel. But I think Mr. Rickey knew, with his almost uncanny ability to analyze the future, that

I was going to need Rae's strength, her warmth, and her wisdom in the days to come.

I now felt that I was in the position to support her and also to take care of my obligations to my mother.

Rae and I agreed to be married as soon as I came back from a South American barnstorming tour and just before I would report to Montreal to either flop on my face or make it big. With her along, I was confident of the result.

Rae went off to New York to work as a nurse for a couple of months and to buy her wedding dress and some other clothes.

I was to pick up the ring in South America.

Rae's mother wanted us to have a big church wedding. So on February 10, 1946, we were married in California. I will always feel sympathy for those poor fellows in the movies who can't find the wedding ring. My best man, Jack Gordon, gave us a few bad moments when he started searching for the ring and couldn't find it right away.

That wasn't the only thing that went wrong.

After the ceremony, as we walked down the aisle together, I recognized some of my old buddies from the Pepper Street Gang in the church. How was I supposed to know it wasn't the thing to interrupt the outgoing wedding march to stop in the aisle and shake hands with old friends. I'd never been married before. Rae kept her head up and marched the rest of the way by herself, waiting for me on the steps outside while I chatted merrily with my friends. She laughs about the whole business now, but I don't think she thought it was funny on our wedding day.

To add to our wedding adventures, one of my practical joker friends had deliberately "borrowed" my car. He finally brought it back. I was so happy to be married that I was able to restrain the urge to clobber him.

From the very beginning of our life together Rae demonstrated the same kind of loving understanding that had always been characteristic of her. She didn't get sore at me when we almost missed getting into the hotel where we were to spend our wedding night—because I had failed to confirm a reservation. She didn't act the part of the injured bride because I hadn't arranged for flowers in our room.

You hear fellows talking about how sweet and considerate a girl can be up until the wedding day, after which she begins to show her true colors. Well, Rae never changed.

It was a good thing she was this kind of girl, because a few weeks after we were married she got an unpleasant sample of the kind of problems she was going to have to share with me.

We were leaving California to fly to Daytona Beach, Florida, where I was to report for spring training with Montreal. En route we had a stopover in New Orleans.

We arrived about seven in the morning, and we were told there would be a short wait. The airlines people informed us we had been bumped off our flight and promised to get us another. This went on for several hours. Finally we asked where we could rest and get some food until our flight problem was straightened out.

The waiting was neither short nor sweet. There was no place where black people could rest at the airport. As for food, if we were willing to buy some sandwiches "to take out," there was a restaurant which would take care of us. Rae and I both felt we would rather starve than be treated in such a humiliating manner.

We left the airport and went to one of the few hotels in which blacks could stay in New Orleans. If I have ever seen an unsanitary "fleabag," that was it. After a few hours, when we couldn't stand the room any longer, we phoned the airport, which had promised to call us. They told us to come over. When we got there, we waited another few hours. At seven o'clock that night, twelve hours after we had arrived, we were told we could get a plane to our destination.

Our troubles weren't over yet. When the plane

landed at Pensacola, we were "bumped" again and white passengers were given our seats. The reason the airport manager gave us was so ridiculous that I won't even repeat it.

The airport people said there was another plane due the next morning but they didn't know whether we could get space on it. I was supposed to report for spring training the following day. I was divided between frustrated anger and anxiety about getting off on the wrong foot in my new career by being late.

Finally the airlines agent ordered a limousine to take us into town where we would be able to find a place to stay and get some kind of transportation to Jacksonville in the morning.

There wasn't even a fleabag hotel in Pensacola where we could register. Somebody told us about a black family that would put us up. That didn't work out. This family lived in a tiny house which could barely accommodate the husband and wife and their large family. They wanted to make room for us but we didn't have the heart to crowd them anymore.

We found there was a bus to Jacksonville within a short time and decided to take it. There weren't many people on the bus. We took our seats, pushed the little buttons which let the chairs back so you can rest or sleep, and got ready to try to relax and forget the unpleasantness and our fatigue. It wasn't long before the driver ordered us to seats at the rear of the bus. These were the seats reserved for people of our race and they didn't have any reclining device. We rode in straight-back chairs. We ate nothing because all that was available were sandwich handouts from the back doors or windows of restaurants where you could spend your money but were not allowed to enter and sit down in comfort.

To be a black man in the South—or other parts of our country where such savage discriminations face you—is bad enough. To have to watch the woman you love and respect treated in such an inhuman way, and to know that there is nothing you can do about it—nothing to protect and shield her, nothing to keep her from bleeding and suffering inside—well, it's almost impossible to find a way to express your feelings. They are mingled with bitterness, with anger, with helplessness, and include just about every negative reaction you can name. You feel a deep sense of personal injury. You also feel a frightening doubt about what has happened to a country which was once the cradle of freedom.

Harry Belafonte often said that if it were not for the great strength of black women—back from the slave days of Phyllis Wheatley and Sojourner Truth and Harriet Tubman right through the age of the late Mary McLeod Bethune, Daisy Bates,

Mrs. Medgar Evers, and Mrs. Martin Luther King, Jr.—the nation would have lost much of its magnificent black leadership. I agree with this. Every time I think of the tremendous contribution a Martin Luther King has made to humanity, I feel people should say a prayer of gratitude for the strength of the mother who bore and nurtured him and the courage of the wife who lived with him in a bomb-threatened and bombarded home.

Back in that New Orleans station, in the fleabag hotel, waiting in an airport with its employees who never intended to serve us, back there on the Jim Crow bus, I could easily have exploded and fought a senseless, losing fight. I could have lost my temper and ended up clobbered unconscious—or worse—in some obscure Southern jail. Maybe this would have happened if it hadn't been for Rae. Acutely conscious of how much Rae was hurt by all the insults and the deprivations, I was also aware that she wanted me to keep a tight grip on myself. She wanted me to take what I had to take so I could survive to do the job ahead. I didn't have to do futile, heroic things to prove to her how much I cared for her. She would have more pride in me if I could follow through on Mr. Rickey's advice to suffer the loss of a few battles so that we could win a war.

8

Making the Grade

AFTER A STAY OF A COUPLE of days at Daytona Beach, Rae and I set out for Sanford, Florida. I was to join two hundred other players of the Brooklyn Dodgers' 1946 farm organization.

We were to stay at the home of a black physician, Dr. Brock.

Rae admitted to me later that she was quite worried that first morning as I prepared to report to the club. She knew there would be many problems and she was hoping I wouldn't let them get me down.

I'm not going to say I wasn't worried.

Mr. Rickey had signed another black player, Johnny Wright, a pitcher, and he was one of the first persons I met. It was encouraging to be welcomed by Clyde Sukeforth, my scout friend. It wasn't too encouraging to get a brief look at the two hundred men with whom I would be in competition. I noted immediately that many of them were Southerners.

When we had drawn our equipment from the clubhouse, I was confronted by what seemed to be a small army of reporters. One of their first questions was whether I thought I could get along with ''these white boys.'' I answered that I had found no problems in getting along with white boys at UCLA, in Pasadena, or in the Army.

''What will you do if one of these pitchers throws at your head?'' I was asked.

I said I would duck, just like anyone else.

One of the newspapermen wanted to know if I had ambitions of becoming a Brooklyn Dodger. I admitted that I had hopes. Another reporter threw me a fast curve.

''Seeing you're going to play shortstop with Montreal, this means you want to become a Dodger and take Pee Wee Reese's job as a short-stop for Brooklyn, doesn't it?''

''I'm not after anyone's job,'' I countered. ''I'm going to do my best to make the team and play where I'm assigned to play. Right now, I haven't got time to think about Brooklyn. I haven't made Montreal yet.''

When I got away from the reporters, Sukeforth introduced me to Clay Hopper, Montreal's manager. There were several things I already knew about Hopper. He was from Mississippi. He owned a plantation, and from what I had been told, he had no great love for blacks.

There was one thing I didn't know. I didn't know that Hopper had begged Mr. Rickey not to send me to this team.

"Please don't do this to me," he had begged. "I'm a white man, been living in Mississippi all my life. If you do this to me, you're going to force me to move out of Mississippi."

Yet here he was on the day I reported, greeting me pleasantly. He told Wright and me that there wouldn't be too much for us to do on our first day. We'd just throw the ball around and hit a few.

On the evening of the second day word came that Mr. Rickey had ordered me back to Daytona Beach.

Well, I thought bitterly, I'm sent here to play shortstop and my stay in Sanford really turns out to be a short stop. Oversensitive and apprehensive, I wondered if the "noble experiment" was being abandoned so soon. I learned the truth a few days later when the rest of the team followed me to Daytona. It seemed the authorities in Sanford had objected strenuously to the mixing of colored and white ballplayers. So Mr. Rickey had made the move to avoid the trouble that was brewing.

In Daytona there was trouble brewing inside of

me. I was overanxious to demonstrate my right to be with Montreal. I went overboard, knocking myself out to impress the Royals manager, Clay Hopper. I began throwing too hard and developed a sore arm. Then I got to the point where I couldn't throw at all and had to take it easy with light workouts at first base.

When the arm recovered, I was assigned to second base.

Thanks to the friendly daily coaching of Lou Rochelli, one of my teammates who voluntarily made me his protégé, I learned a lot about approaching base, taking the shortstop's throw, getting rid of the ball, and hurdling the runner. As an infielder, except at shortstop, I was beginning to show something.

That something wasn't enough. My hitting record was atrocious. I didn't hit in Montreal practice games, nor when the Royals visited the Dodgers. In a solid month of training I came up with only two or three decisive hits.

At first my failure was excused on the grounds that I was in a state of high tension and reacting to terrific pressure. After that first month had gone by, the I-told-you-soers got to work. One sports writer sneered: ''It's do-gooders like Rickey that hurt the Negro because they try to force inferior Negroes on whites and then everybody loses. If he were white they'd have booted him out of camp long ago.''

Mr. Rickey took personal command in this crisis. He left Dodger camp and joined us. He invited Rae to come to practice, hoping to provide me with more inspiration. He himself stood by the base line and urged me on with mumbled instructions to be more daring, to run with all I had, to gamble more, to take a bigger lead.

Throughout all these first days of trial and error I was doing my best to keep my mind removed from the racial implications of my situation. Yet I couldn't forget our being forced out of Sanford. I wondered how strong the pressures were to get Mr. Rickey to back down. I hoped he wouldn't. Nothing bad had happened to me personally yet, except that Rae and I—in both Daytona and Sanford—were lodged in private black homes while all the rest of the team lived in hotels. This separation was something we had known we must face, yet the advance knowledge still didn't make it easy to accept.

There were times when I brooded over the price one had to pay because of skin color, but one of the things that helped me out of my depression was the reaction of my own people in Sanford and in Daytona Beach. They turned out in droves to watch the practice games, and they communicated to me by their cheers, their shouted words of encouragement, and the pride which glowed in their eyes that they were counting on me to deliver.

I couldn't let them down. I had to justify their faith.

The night before the first game between the Dodgers and the Royals I was as nervous as a cat. The rumor mill had it circulating that I would be pulled out of the game. What the rumor mongers didn't know was that Mr. Rickey had done some efficient, behind-the-scenes negotiating with city officials.

When I walked out on the field, I was ready to take the booing, the bad names, all the resentment I thought I would have to face. Instead, I encountered no unpleasantness except a few scattered boos.

Maybe this wonderful surprise was the factor which gave me the morale, from my position at second, to intercept a hot grounder which looked like a sure hit. My arm was fine. My legs carried me faster than I knew I could run. I captured the ball and flung it hard, forcing the runner coming down from first.

During the next few days, both at practice and in intra-squad games, I came through with similar plays. Branch Rickey was overjoyed. So was Rae.

It was such a big thing to her that one evening she cooked a special dinner and we had a gay little celebration with some of the black reporters.

A lot of theories have been advanced—some of them incredibly imaginative and inaccurate—about why and how I loosened up and relaxed to the point where I could really begin hitting. Those were such days of stress that I can't put my finger on what actually brought about the change, but it came.

One thing I shall never forget in this connection was the encouragement and help I received from Clyde Sukeforth, the scout who had contacted me originally in behalf of Mr. Rickey. He was constantly around, doing and saying anything he thought might sharpen my morale and improve my work.

During this period one of my biggest and most inspiring days came when the Royals played their first game in Jersey City. Hopper had shown his confidence in me by assigning me to second base. I was ready and anxious to accept the challenge.

We held the Jersey City team scoreless in the second inning. In our half of the third it didn't take long to prove that I could produce in the clutch. With two men on base, I swung and connected. You know when you have hit a good one. The cheers of the crowd told me that the ball had gone all the way. In fact, it had flown 340 feet over the left-field fence. It was my first home run in major league baseball. I think I was the happiest man in the world. In the midst of all the excitement and exhibition, I somehow managed to search the wildly yelling fans and telescope Rae's face. You can imagine how happy she was and how thrilled I was that I had made her happy.

I don't know what I appreciated most—my own sense of fulfillment, Rae's reaction, the approval of the crowd, or the warm praise which was given to me by my fellow players, the Southern fellows as well as the others. The response of my teammates was so important. I had to be accepted by them before I could truly consider myself—or be considered—a real Dodger.

I was just hitting my stride with Jersey City. The next time at bat, with the memory of the home run, I decided to lay a bunt down third base. It was perfectly executed. I beat it out for a hit. I got the sign to steal second, got a very good jump on the pitcher, and made it easily.

This opening day in Jersey City produced much more for us than anyone had expected. I had made four hits, a home run, and three singles, with two bases stolen along the way. The crowd demonstrated its appreciation with loud cheers and applause as I walked off the field.

"Mr. Rickey," I was saying in my mind, "you

were right. The fans won't care about your color if you give them proof that you can be colorful and daring—and a winner.''

The three games at Jersey City were triumphant experiences. The "wait and see-ers," the trouble predictors, were warning that the worst was yet to come. Baltimore was our next stop. And Baltimore turned out to be pretty rough.

Name-calling, which had been sneaky in Florida, was indulged in with great abandon there. I shudder when I think of the foul things Rae had to listen to, coming from fans directly behind her. But the trouble ended there. The violence which had been predicted and the boycotts which had been threatened just didn't come off.

On the contrary, the attendance was very good. As had happened in Jersey City, black fans also turned out in amazing numbers, and the story was beginning to get around that use of a black in organized baseball was not only morally right but also financially beneficial.

It was like a breath of free air to leave for Montreal. There Rae and I tasted what it feels like not only to be accepted but respected and wanted. The people of Montreal were wonderful. They really made us feel at home, even if it seemed sometimes as if we were living in a home fashioned of glass. People stared at us on the street. Youngsters followed us everywhere we went. Their curiosity was of the warm, friendly kind, with admiration mixed in. We had no housing problem. We were able to rent a charming apartment. It was a happy time for us, especially because Rae was going to become a mother.

Following the Montreal idyll, we hit the road again, traveling to Baltimore, Syracuse, Newark, Jersey City, Toronto, Buffalo, and Rochester. It is a matter of record that one of the most painful experiences I encountered occurred not in the deep South but in upstate New York, in Syracuse.

A wise guy from the Syracuse team trotted out a black cat on the field, shouting that this was my cousin. Sometimes when I boiled up inside and couldn't take it out any other way, I got even by playing my very best. Right after the childish black cat insult, I ripped a double down left field. As I raced past them, I called out to the Syracuse team, "I'll bet my cousin's pretty happy now, huh?"

The lines were beginning to crack along newspaper row. More and more the sports columnists began to admit that the Rickey experiment seemed destined for success. Still, there were the "incidents."

I remember the rough time I faced when we

went to Louisville after our team had won the pennant. A pretty vile stream of abuse came at me from the bleachers. Whether this experience had anything to do with it or not, I don't know, but I slumped again until we went to Montreal, where we would have to rack up three out of four to win the playoff for the Little World Series. Louisville represented the American Association and we represented the International League. We made it three straight in Montreal. I hit .400 and scored the winning run in the final game. I tried not to exult over the fact that the Montreal fans, having heard of the bad time Louisville had given our team, gave it back hot and heavy to the Louisville boys. These wonderfully loyal Canadians had many loud boos for the Louisville visitors. To turn the tables even more decisively, the Montreal fans mobbed onto the field after the game and carried Clay Hopper, Curt Davis, our pitcher, and me around the field for half an hour. As a matter of fact, I was chased by friendly fans all the way to my hotel.

As we left the dressing room, we knew the fans were still out there, yelling and expressing their pleasure. Someone had arranged to get a car to take Rae and me home. She was waiting in the car. I had to break through that friendly crowd to get to the car, and even after I did, they were chasing the moving vehicle. I think it was Wendell Smith, then of the Pittsburgh *Courier,* who wrote that it was the first time in history that a black American had been chased by a mob out of love instead of hate.

The Montreal victory made me very happy. I was even happier to realize that Manager Clay Hopper's attitude toward me had changed to a very positive one. It was a tribute to his power of self-control and restraint that I had not realized how bitterly he had questioned himself about my right to be on the team. I found out, for instance, that very early in the season he had made an amazing remark to Mr. Rickey. The two men were standing together on one occasion when I executed a difficult play.

Mr. Rickey turned to Hopper.

"That was a superhuman play!" he exulted.

Hopper responded with a question.

"Mr. Rickey," he asked, "do you really think a nigger's a human being?"

Fortunately for me, I didn't hear about this until much later. When Mr. Rickey told me the story, sometime afterward, he recalled that he had turned on Hopper to make an angry retort but had choked it off.

"I saw that this Mississippi-born man was sincere, that he meant what he said; that this attitude of regarding the black as subhuman was part of his heritage; that here was a man who had practically nursed race prejudice from his mother's breast. So I decided to ignore the question," Mr. Rickey told me.

Mr. Rickey was right. This was the same man who was to say to me, at the end of the season: "Jackie, you're a real ballplayer and a gentleman. It's been wonderful having you on the team."

Spring training was set up for the Dodgers and Royals in Cuba in 1947. The Royals now had three more Negro players: Roy Campanella, Don Newcombe, and Roy Partlow. We had to live Jim Crow in Havana because Mr. Rickey felt sure we were on the brink of cracking the opposition to blacks in the majors. He didn't want to take any chance of causing incidents at this crucial point.

I had spent the whole previous season learning second base, and just when I thought I was making progress, along came another Rickey order which disturbed me and made me feel quite uncertain. I was to learn first base in preparation for a Dodger assignment. This meant I would have to start all over again, learing a position I wasn't sure I could handle.

Mr. Rickey's strategy—assigning the black players to separate quarters in Cuba and shifting me to first base with Montreal—was designed to keep down dissension. He wanted to put me in the spotlight where I could show so well that the Dodgers themselves would be crying for me to move up to their team.

Someone tried to throw a monkey wrench into the works.

The reassignment to first base was a tip-off to the Dodgers. They realized now that Rickey meant business when he said he was going to bring me up to their team. Some of the Brooklyn players, opposed to the idea, decided to get up a petition saying they would refuse to play with me on the team. The Dodger boss stepped on that one fast and hard. He called in the ringleaders and let them know that they could sign all the petitions they wanted. He wouldn't back down. Furthermore, anyone who felt he couldn't tolerate playing with a black need not feel obligated to stay. With all the other opposition Mr. Rickey anticipated, he wasn't having any revolt on his own home base. The revolt crumbled as revolts usually do when met with firmness and decisive courage.

When the Dodger-Royal games came up in Panama, I hit .625, stole seven bases, and did a pretty fair job at first. After breaking camp in April, we were to have a two-day series in Brooklyn the week before the season opened. Mr.

Rickey was prepared to make his historic announcement, preceded by a well-planned statement to the press from Manager Leo Durocher of the Dodgers. Durocher would be doing the spadework to cushion the shock.

There was another hitch. On April 9, 1947, the opening game was called because of rain. Following that, everyone was thunderstruck to learn that Durocher had been suspended for "conduct detrimental to baseball," as the official charges put it. The suspension was for one year.

To turn the spotlight away from Durocher's suspension, during the game against the Dodgers at Ebbets Field, right after I had bunted into a double play for Montreal, reporters in the press box were handed sheets of paper on which one cryptic line appeared. This one line served notice that I had just finished my last game for the Montreal team. It read:

"The Brooklyn Dodgers today purchased the contract of Jackie Robinson from Montreal."

9

Breakthrough to the Big League

LESS THAN A WEEK AFTER I joined the Brooklyn club, I played in my first game against the Braves. We won 5–3 but I didn't cover myself with glory. In fact I didn't do well at all that day. I was in another one of those horrible slumps. Playing first base, I grounded to the third baseman in the first inning, flied out to left field, hit into a double play, was safe on error, and later in the game was removed as a defensive safeguard.

I did get one hit.

I am certain the sellout crowd at Ebbets Field was disappointed. I know I was.

I imagine there were some curiosity seekers at that game who had come anticipating trouble because of my presence. They were disappointed. My fellow Dodgers were neither friendly nor hostile. And the Boston boys took everything in stride.

Branch Rickey had been looking around for

Robinson made his major league debut on Opening Day, 1947.

someone to replace the benched Leo Durocher. He selected Burt Shotten, who came out of retirement to take over the club.

In that season—1947—it was generally believed that it was Brooklyn's year for the pennant. We had a pretty terrific team. As pitchers there were Ralph Branca, Hank Behrman, Vic Lombardi, Rex Barney, Harry Taylor, Joe Hatten, and in the bullpen, Hugh Casey.

Bruce Edwards was catching; Dixie Walker, Pete Reiser, and Gene Hermanski rotated with Carl Furillo in the outfield. Johnny Jorgensen and Cookie Lavagetto held down third base. Pee Wee Reese was shortstop, Ed Stanky at second, and yours truly on first. In the batting order I was second behind Stanky, the lead-off man.

Manager Shotten and I got along very well, hitting it off right from the beginning.

But not all the news was good.

Ironically the first big ordeal I was put through in the majors wasn't the work of a deep South team. The Philadelphia Phillies were the first to create ugliness in my major league career.

We had met our old rivals, the Giants, at the Polo Grounds and given them a 10–4 drubbing. We were in pretty good shape psychologically when the Phillies came to Ebbets Field.

I went to bat in the first inning. As I started

toward home plate, members of Ben Chapman's team (our visitors) began shouting insults:

"Go back to the bushes, black boy."

"Hey, nigger. Go back where you came from."

"They're waiting for you in the jungles. We don't want you here, black boy."

I churned up inside but I was prepared. This was the kind of thing Mr. Rickey had foreseen. I wasn't going to let them get the best of me.

The little compliments increased in volume and in profanity as the game went on. I began to notice that my teammates, who up until now had been so noncommittal, were starting to get angry at the Philly bullies.

Ed Stanky, our second baseman, called time and ran over to me.

"Jack," he said, "play this fellow a little closer to the bag."

I believe it was the first time Stanky had given me advice.

"Thanks," I told Ed.

"By the way," he said, patting me on the back, "don't let those bums get you down."

I felt much better prepared for whatever I must take.

The first seven innings were scoreless. We got the Phillies out in the eighth and our team came to bat.

I led off. The insults came from the Phillies' dugout once more.

I let the first pitch go by for a ball and slammed the next one into center field for a single.

The Phillies' pitcher, being a knuckle ball expert, gave me no advantage and I stole second early. Gene Hermanski came up to hit and I took my lead off first. As the Phillies' pitcher let fly, I lit out for second base. On the throw it was wide and bounced past the shortshop as I moved into third. Hermanski singled me home and that decided the ball game.

I felt that the name callers had been answered.

Another answer came from the press. Columnists and editorial writers severely lashed Chapman. In self-defense the Phillies manager hurriedly called a press conference to explain that, although the name-calling had taken place, his men were not anti-black. It seemed they had hurled all this filth at me for the good of my soul. Such treatment, Chapman explained, would make me grow to major league stature. That was the way the Phillies played ball, Chapman said. They had called DiMaggio ''the Wop'' and Whitey Kurowski ''the Polack.''

Many people viewed this explanation as a clumsy cover-up. Baseball Commissioner Happy Chandler warned the Phillies to change their habits.

There was one person who wasn't angry with Chapman. Branch Rickey, who usually could see far beyond the obvious, commented happily: "Chapman did more than anybody to make Dixie Walker, Eddie Stanky, and other Dodgers speak up in Robinson's behalf. When he poured out that stream of abuse, he solidified and unified thirty men, not one of whom was willing to sit by and see someone kick a man around who had his hands tied behind his back. Chapman created in Robinson's behalf a thing called sympathy—the most unifying word in the world. That word has a Greek origin; it means to suffer. Thus, to say 'I sympathize with you' means 'I suffer with you.' That is what Chapman did. He caused men like Stanky to suffer with Robinson and he made this Negro a real member of the Dodgers."

As a result of the Chapman incident, I had to submit myself to one of the toughest ordeals I ever faced. I agreed to pose for a picture with Chapman to make the fans feel that we had patched up our differences. My heart wasn't in it. In addition to my lack of respect for Chapman as a man, I learned that when he was asked to pose with me, he agreed on condition that he wouldn't have to shake hands with me and could pose with both of us standing together holding a baseball bat. The only reason I went along with this piece of hypocrisy was that Mr. Rickey sincerely believed it would help the game and the position of blacks in baseball.

As you can well imagine, things like the Chapman incident were especially hard to take. I don't believe I would have been able to make it in such a tense situation if it hadn't been for the help and guidance I received from two people. These two individuals helped me to maintain control and to concentrate on the positive effort to win friends. From them I learned to avoid being constantly on the defensive, to reject the conclusion that everyone was a potential enemy.

The two people, of course, were Branch Rickey and my wife, Rae. Mr. Rickey's voice and his words were constantly with me. His admonition to "turn the other cheek" came back to me at crucial moments. As for Rae, she was just superb from the beginning. I can remember so often coming home, after a bad day back in Montreal, when I had run into some kind of difficulty. There were times when I believed I was on the verge of a nervous breakdown. I remember the comforting words Rae would say and the way she kissed me. It was that sensitive instinct she had, knowing exactly the right thing to say or do at crucial times, that helped me come back out of any depression.

Much of the strength I got came from my own Dodger teammates. Some of them helped without saying a word—merely by the way they accepted me as a member of the team. Others went so far as to reassure me that they accepted me. There is one ex-teammate of mine whom I will never forget because he was one of the pioneers in speaking up for me when I couldn't speak up for myself.

I am talking about Pee Wee Reese, the talented Brooklyn shortstop. Pee Wee's support of me was particularly significant, because as I have mentioned, when I first joined the Montreal Royals as shortstop, some sports writer hinted that I was after Reese's job.

Pee Wee's background made it perfectly natural for him to oppose integrated baseball. He was from Louisville, Kentucky, the same city that gave me such a hard time when I was with Montreal playing against Louisville in the Little World Series. Pee Wee told me his family had expressed some concern about his playing with me. Yet from the very beginning he took a positive attitude about my coming to the Dodgers. Early in my first season with Brooklyn Reese told a friend that he realized some of his friends in Louisville wouldn't like the idea of his playing with a black. He didn't care about that, he said.

"I never met Jackie Robinson," Reese told reporters, "but I believe he deserves a chance just like anyone else. I've thought about it a great deal and I've tried to put myself in his place. I said to myself; "Suppose Negroes were in the majority in this country and for years they had barred white players. Then, suppose someone gave me a chance to be the first white player on a Negro team. I'd be so lonely and scared and I sure would appreciate a guy who didn't go out of his way to kick me in the teeth." So, when I put myself in Robinson's place, I made up my mind that I wasn't going to be the one to give him any kicks in the teeth."

About my possibly taking his job, Pee Wee's answer was: "There may be enough room in baseball for both of us."

I'll always be grateful that not only was there enough room in baseball for both Pee Wee Reese and Jackie Robinson, but also that he was my teammate and partner on the field. I can tell you that Reese's friendship, his courage in expressing it, and his ability to sense my burdens really fortified me.

I needed that kind of help. Mr. Rickey had been accurate in his predictions of unpleasantness. There was name-calling by fans and by other players. There were snubs and insults. There were viciously pitched balls, aimed at my head. In the early days of my career I won the doubtful distinction of being hit by more of those than any other batter in the league. There were letters containing threats to hurt my wife, to kill me, to do harm to our baby son, little Jackie, Jr. Crank letters, the police called them. But how was one to know? There were official statements from the Ku Klux Klan, hinting what would happen to me if I came to a certain Dixie town to play ball.

All this was the public part of the abuse which Mr. Rickey had known I would have to face.

There was also a private part.

How cruelly stupid, it seemed, to be living at the center of a group of guys, fighting with them every step of the way during the ball game, and then, when the game was over and you were back in the locker rooms, to find yourself off in your little corner while the rest of the fellows joked and exulted over a victory or tried to mend each other's morale after a defeat. In the early days, after the game was over, you didn't see your teammates until time to go back to work. They lived in their world and you lived in yours. They lived in the best hotels in town and you lived, maybe, with a private family. Their wives knew each other and were friends. You and your wife got an invitation once in a while to someone's home for dinner or went to a black movie house. On trains you sat by yourself or with a black newspaperman who might be along. On trains the others played cards and you watched or pretended to be reading a book or a newspaper.

There were times when I felt deeply sorry for myself about these conditions, times when I was humiliated for my wife and child, times when I wondered if the cost of being the first black in the majors was going to be worth the reward. There were times when I couldn't sleep or felt so nauseated that I couldn't eat. I was often physically and mentally whipped and worst of all, although I tried to prevent it, sometimes the punishment I was taking was reflected in my performance on the field. I think what hurt me most was getting into a slump. I'd be willing to take practically anything if only I could play ball so well that my teammates, the opposition, the fans, the writers, the bosses of the game—and everyone—would have to admit that Branch Rickey had been right. I couldn't be mediocre or just good. I had to be great, if I had the capacity.

I often think back to the times I watched my teammates playing cards and wished I could be part of the game. But one day one of the fellows simply invited me to sit down and join in.

There was one occasion when an ugly incident could have occurred. We were playing cards on the train. Hugh Casey, the Southern-born relief pitcher, startled everyone by declaring:

"Tell you what I used to do down in Georgia when my poker luck got bad. I'd just get up and go out and I'd rub me the biggest, blackest nigger woman I could find." He reached over and rubbed my head.

For a second I sat in the tense silence. "Mr. Rickey," I was saying to myself, "I'm sorry, Mr. Rickey. But here goes the *real* Jackie Robinson. No red-blooded Negro lets a white man insult him like this."

The next second I heard the echo of that rumbling voice in Brooklyn.

"I'm looking for a ballplayer, Jackie, with guts enough *not* to fight back." In a blinding flash that cut through my rising anger I saw that if I lost my temper there would be headlines which would give aid and comfort to everyone who had opposed integration in baseball and cause humiliation to all those who had fought for it.

Quietly I told the man holding the cards to deal.

The tension broke. The game continued. A few days later my teammates had to hold Hugh Casey back because he wanted to rush out on the field to crucify a St. Louis Cardinal player who had spiked me.

Just to keep the record straight, I didn't feel vindicated for having taken Casey's insult just because Casey gave me this approval afterward.

No, there was something much more important
at stake than Casey's approval. I was an exhibit in
a glass cage—a tiger who had been trained not to
roar. The day would come when I could roar as
loudly as I wished and whenever I pleased.
Maybe during these days when I couldn't fight
back I could help to fix it so there would be less to
roar about in days to come.

Coming back to Pee Wee Reese: Reese not only
did things to help ease my private situation; he
proved more than once his willingness to put it on
the line for me in public. The incident I remember
best happened in Boston. By that time Reese and
I had become a much talked about double-play
combination. In Boston we went out to take our
infield practice for the first time in that city. Some
of the Boston players began to kid Pee Wee. There
wasn't anything vicious about their quips—not as
vicious as some of the remarks and insults which
had been made by players in other cities. The
Boston fellows were kidding Reese, riding him
about being from Louisville and playing ball with
a black. They shouted derisive questions about
what this white boy from Louisville and his black
buddy were going to do after the game.

After a few minutes of this Pee Wee, who
hadn't answered a word, left his position and
walked over to mine. He didn't even look at the
jeering Boston team. He placed his hand on my

shoulder and began talking to me. I don't think either one of us knew at that time or remembered later what we talked about. But what Pee Wee was saying to the Boston boys by his simple gesture was this:

"Yell! Do anything you please. We came here to play baseball. As long as Jackie Robinson does all he possibly can as a ball player to help the Brooklyn club win games, that is all we are asking."

From that minute on there wasn't any more kidding about Pee Wee and me. There were, however, many attempts to drive a wedge between us.

In spite of them, we became close friends—two guys who could talk frankly about how silly it was for anyone to hate anyone else for his color. Pee Wee even asked me to meet the members of his family who had been opposed to our friendship.

By placing the emphasis on what Reese did to help bring about good will among the Dodgers, I do not mean to slight others on the Brooklyn club who became convinced that they, too, had a contribution to make. Reese was just one of the first and the most constant. I can't forget Ed Stanky, our second baseman when I became a Dodger. From the beginning he was giving me tips about various opposing players, encouraging me, and exhibiting genuine friendship. And Clyde Sukeforth, the scout who had brought me in, also proved most helpful. He did all he could to see me through.

Yet to me Reese and Branch Rickey symbolize the answer to the differences and the hatreds between people. Mr. Rickey and Reese were the leaders in making a great experiment work. Mr. Rickey had the courage to put me up front. Reese had the daring and the integrity to back me up, leading the way to good will between me and my fellow players.

I mentioned Ed Stanky before. I remember once, during a particularly nasty exhibition on the part of the opposing team, I was being shouted at and insulted and called every conceivable name.

I didn't reply. Ed Stanky did.

"You yellow-bellied cowards!" Stanky shouted. "Why don't you yell at someone who can answer back?"

Stanky had asked a question which heralded the crack of dawn Branch Rickey had envisioned when he predicted: "The day when your team-mates take up the fight for you, that is the day we will have begun to win the battle of integration in baseball."

Back in May of 1947—my first year with the Brooklyn club—we found out how desperate people can become when they are eaten up with hate. A threat which did not involve our personal safety, but which could have wrecked my career, became news that May.

Stanley Woodward of The New York *Herald Tribune* scooped the country by exposing a protest strike planned by members of the St. Louis Cardinals. The plot was that when our team went to play there, they would refuse to play because I was a Dodger. The article stated that some of the Cardinals were attempting to spread such tactics throughout the league to try to keep blacks out of the game.

Ford Frick, president of the National League, stepped on that one—and fast. Woodward wrote that Frick had informed the players involved that they would be suspended from the league if any such plan materialized.

"You will find that the friends you think you have in the press box will not support you, that you will be outcasts," Frick threatened. "I do not care if half the league strikes. Those who do it will encounter quick retribution. They will be suspended and I don't care if it wrecks the National League for five years. This is the United States of America and one citizen has as much right to play as another.

"The National League will go down the line with Robinson whatever the consequence. You will find if you go through with your intention that you have been guilty of complete madness."

That was that.

But if St. Louis had been tamed, there was to be more heard from Philadelphia.

We were beginning a series of games with the Phillies in Shibe Park. During the first game the Phillies again began their name-calling tactics—only with more vehemence this time. They had help from some of the local fans who decided to get into the act.

The second incident with the Phillies brought another official warning from Frick.

"I don't expect Philadelphia or any other team to handle Jackie Robinson with kid gloves," Frick told Philly Manager Chapman, "but let's keep the blows above the belt."

I'll never know to what extent the weight of all these pressures affected my game. I do know that I was in a horrible batting slump. Early in the season, out of twenty-one times at bat, I only got one hit.

I was frightened by my failure to produce. I heard rumors that I was going to be benched. Luckily for me, however, both Branch Rickey and Burt Shotten had faith that I would come through.

My old "friends," the Phillies, returned to our home field. There was something about these fellows that really inspired. I felt some of the old power returning, and in the third game of the series I broke through.

In the fourth inning the Phillies were leading 2–0. Leading off, I singled to left field. Four straight hits, followed, producing three runs.

Both teams scored later, and in the eighth I had a homer, giving us the insurance run that we needed to move us into third place. We didn't look back from there until we had won the pennant.

I had begun to gain a new confidence. When I joined Montreal, in the beginning of it all, I had a reputation for stealing bases. But with the Dodgers I had held myself down to orthodox patterns. In a night game in Pittsburgh, near the end of June, with the score tied at 2–2, I watched Pitcher Fritz Ostermuller closely. From where I fidgeted at third he appeared to me to be getting a little too relaxed. Something told me to break loose. I danced off third cautiously. Ostermuller wound up, paying me no attention. The pitch was a ball. I eased open my lead off third. When Ostermuller began his windup, I tore out for home plate and slid in safe, loving the roars from the stands.

The stolen run put us out front, 3–2. Some of the Dodgers, excited and happy, came to meet me with congratulations as I ran to the bench.

The slump was over. One of the best indications that the club was no longer worried about my not being able to come through was that Schultz, a player who had been mentioned as my possible replacement when it appeared that I might be benched, was sold by the club. It looked as though I would be around the Brooklyn club for a while.

Some people never want to give up. I've told how the Phillies kept trying to "get" me. The St. Louis Cardinals had their own special brand of persistence. They hadn't been able to get away with the planned strike, but some, though not all, of the players were determined to do something to make things unpleasant.

The St. Louis club came to Brooklyn for a series with us. In the eleventh, Enos Slaughter, the Cardinals' outfielder, spiked me rather cruelly. Fortunately the injury did not prove serious.

The indignation of my fellow Dodgers over the spiking was very deep and I honestly believe that this feeling was one of the factors which helped bring all of us closer together, united in a fierce determination to answer this kind of sportsmanship with a triumph for our team that season.

I was grateful for the fellowship which began to develop among my fellow players and me.

One thing that had made things tough for me

at the beginning was that I had a chip on my shoulder when I first came into the game.

I allowed the newspapers to make me pre-judge the fellows I would be playing with. Back there in 1945 and 1946 the press was saying that the Brooklyn players would not tolerate my presence on the team. There were reams of copy written—some guesses, some derived from actual interview—to the effect that the Dodger members just couldn't bring themselves to be part of inter-racial baseball. When I first came up on the team, I stayed in my own little corner. I was afraid to try to associate with my teammates. I imagined that there would be riots and fights and that the fellows on the team would do all kinds of vicious things. It didn't take me long to realize that I was wrong. If we were to be successful, I had, in some way, to get along with the fellows in the ball club, to get them to know and understand me. I couldn't expect them to take the giant step all by themselves to create a friendship with me. I had to walk some of the way, too.

With our stronger team spirit we managed to get even with Enos Slaughter and the Cardinals for the spiking I had suffered.

In the next three games we played with them in the series, I got a home run, a double, and four singles in thirteen times at bat—a .462 average. We won two of the three.

At the end of my first season as a Dodger I had played in 151 games, scored 125 runs, hit safely 175 times, batted .297, hit 12 home runs, and led the team in stolen bases.

The *Sporting News,* which had been so negative about the chances of a black making good in major league baseball, named me "Rookie of the Year."

I was proud of this, of course, but I was even prouder that a fight had been won—a fight with myself for self-control. And a firm step forward had been taken not only to bring blacks into big-league baseball, but also to bring the kind of democracy to the sport which fair-minded people believed America's pastime should have.

There was still a long way to go—for me personally and for those die-hards who were still opposing the idea. There were so many other people who deserved credit, people like the Wendell Smiths and Billy Rowes who were on the firing line as newspapermen right at the very beginning; people like the black ministers and white sociologists and committee folk who kept knocking at the door until it opened just enough to let the first man through; people like Ford Frick and Clay Hopper and players like Stanky and Reese. And Branch Rickey, of course, and Rae Robinson.

But the fight wasn't over.

10

My "Emancipation" Begins

WE LOST THE 1947 WORLD SERIES to the Yankees. This was a great disappointment but, on the other hand, it was thrilling to our team to have landed on top of the heap so that we could compete in the Series. It had been many years since Brooklyn had climbed that far.

For me, having the opportunity to compete in the World Series was the major thrill of my life. I wasn't even able to sleep the night before the opening game. Imagine how I felt. I was just a rookie. I had only one season of organized base-ball behind me. My nerves remained taut until the first ball was pitched that first day. Although we didn't win, I didn't feel disappointed because I knew each one of us had put forth our very best individual effort. There was another factor which I found very gratifying.

We could have lost all the games in sight, but there was one truth obvious to the public. I was no longer a loner—no longer the one guy on trial.

I had a team backing me up. I was accepted by this team. When I went into baseball, they took me because they had to. Branch Rickey made them. But now I was as important to each one of them as each one of them was to me. This was the real victory.

During my second season—1948—Pee Wee Reese and I became a two-man team within our team. Pee Wee was at shortstop and I had been moved to second base. We worked together for a few weeks until we had perfected a technique in which we complemented each other. This relationship was very satisfying to me. I can't say I was too well satisfied with my record that season. I made the bad mistake of reporting for duty overweight.

I had been at a playing weight of about 192. I came back to camp weighing 220. Leo Durocher was back at the helm, having replaced Shotten. Leo was furious. He had a right to be, but instead of telling me directly, he carried his story to the press; and the way it came out, it sounded as though I had allowed one successful season in baseball to go to my head.

I was pretty sore at the way Leo had handled this and I retaliated by telling my own story to the press. I didn't try to excuse myself for having been careless, but I defended myself against any implication of swell-headedness and said I was taking off weight as fast as possible.

Leo and I have several characteristics in common. We react fairly quickly and we both sound off when we feel justified. There have been a lot of stories around that we don't like each other. The argument over my weight contributed to the belief that we had a feud going. This wasn't true. I believe we have always shared a mutual respect.

Leo gave me the business in spring training. He rode me hard. He could be very sarcastic and he really got to me several times, but I took it because I knew I had been wrong and also that he was doing it not out of spite but because he is a good manager who passionately wants to win.

I got another jolt from Mr. Rickey when I learned that he had put me on the waivers list of players for sale—for $10,000. I was shocked and hurt until I learned that he had no idea of selling my contract. Possibly he wanted to see how the market was for a black and he could have been using this method to reprimand me for being careless about my weight. Maybe it sounds as if I'm making a Federal case about the weight business. Well, let me tell you, it is a serious thing for a major league player to let himself go. If I had reported to camp overweight in 1946 or 1947, I never would have made it in the majors.

There was one bright spot in that 1948 season. You might characterize it as icing on the cake. When we played exhibition games below the Mason-Dixon Line, the attendance was record-breaking. In Fort Worth, Texas, close to sixteen thousand persons turned out one Sunday. In Dallas, Texas, almost twelve thousand came. The Dallas crowd was about 50 per cent black. We saw in the success of these games that the Southern white community was losing its resistance to mixed teams. We also saw that blacks would support major league baseball if it was run along democratic lines.

I had virtually starved off some of my over-weight, dropping fifteen pounds in two weeks. I had ten more to go. The sports writers kept after me about my physical condition, and Leo was still griping.

To make matters worse, I was developing a sore arm.

The first few weeks we were a real bomb as a ball club. I felt awful because I believed a lot of the responsibility was mine.

Gradually the day-to-day play was bringing me around, even though at the age of twenty-nine you don't lose weight so easily. I began hitting again.

There was another serious setback, however. In Cincinnati I collided with Ben Zientara of the

Reds on the first-base line. Zientara was knocked unconscious and I strained my left knee tendons so badly that I was unable to play for a few days.

This accident threw my game back into the miserable state which I had just overcome. The entire team was playing badly and by the end of May the Dodgers' hopes were really low.

It was at this point that Branch Rickey and Horace Stoneham, president of the Giants, made a deal which took Durocher away from Brooklyn. Leo became manager of the Giants.

This created a peculiar situation. The Brooklyn team and the Giants had been bitter rivals for years. Now here was Brooklyn's manager going over to them. To make matters more curious, the Giants had never failed to advertise their lack of love for Leo.

Burt Shotten returned to take over the Dodger team. Ironically, almost as soon as he came back, I got back into stride, conquering weight problems and recovering verve in playing. Naturally Leo believed that I had been holding out on the job for him but was putting out for Shotten because we got along well.

We improved under Shotten, but there was no way to reach the top that 1948 season. We finished third behind Boston and St. Louis.

I have often heard this question: ''In the early days of your career—and up until you had established a record in baseball—how did you manage to curb your temper, the instinct to fight back when attacked or insulted?"

In previous chapters I have tried to point out all the factors which helped me to "turn the other cheek," as Mr. Rickey had counseled me to do.

There was one vital factor I have not mentioned yet. I would say it was as important as any other single thing, and enabled me to take whatever came my way.

Throughout all that seemingly endless period of being called names, facing snubs, insults, threats, and sneak physical attacks, I was living for the day when I could step out of the freak role—that of the first black in the major leagues. I was waiting and praying for the first time when I could react naturally, explosively, if necessary, whenever I felt someone was treating me unfairly.

So long as there was organized opposition by players, fans, and the people who ran baseball, I could not be myself. Until that opposition had been beaten, I had to take every knock and pretend to like it. One of the most effective ways to beat this opposition would be by proving myself on the scoreboards and at the box office. I would have to be able to demonstrate without contradiction that I was an asset to the game. Only then could I learn the luxury of standing up on my own two feet and giving back as good as I received.

The day I could sound off at a player on the opposing team who was riding me or my teammates, the day I could challenge the umpire when I thought he was making an unfair decision, that would be the day of my "emancipation."

That day came at the beginning of the 1949 season.

Branch Rickey, who had schooled me in the art of crawling off into a corner to lie down with my wounds, now told me I was on my own. Mr. Rickey was wise in the ways of winning. Just as he had used the take-it-lying-down method to put his point across, he also had strategic reasons when he "emancipated" me.

"This young man had come through with courage beyond what I ever could have asked," Mr. Rickey told someone. "Yet I knew that burning inside him was the same pride and determination that burned inside those Negro slaves a century earlier and had made them rise up to shout that they were slaves no longer. I knew there were many in baseball who could not understand the reasons behind Robinson's turning the other cheek. They could be made to respect only the fierce competition, the fighting back, the things that are the signs of courage to men who know courage only in its physical sense. That's why I told Robinson he was on his own. Then I sat back happily, knowing that, with the restraints removed, he was going to show the National League a thing or two."

It was amazing—the things that happened when I began acting naturally, being myself.

Some of the very people who had been patting me on the shoulder and some newspaper people who had been marveling at the passive role I had played and saying what a shame it all was—those same people sent up a big howl of resentment when I began asserting myself. They hung labels on me such as "ingrate," "troublemaker," "pop-off" and "rabble rouser." I didn't care about that as long as I felt justified in sounding off. As long as I knew that I wasn't doing things simply to retaliate for the past, I was willing to be called all the names anyone could dream up. I suppose some of these people thought I was always setting up a holler because I felt persecuted as a black. I didn't think that way at all. Not all the opposition I faced was due to race. It's just a fact that riding your opponent, needling him, teasing and ridicul-ing, are as much part and parcel of the American sports concept as hot dogs are American. In every phase of sports there are many instances when people win not only because they show a superior skill, but also because they have perfected a technique of rattling the opposition, getting to him, getting under his skin. Sometimes you defeat this kind of tactic by ignoring it and keeping cool. Other times you win out by sending back better than you are receiving.

I'm not going to go into all the numerous hassles, scrapes, rhubarbs, and controversies in which I became involved after my "emancipation." I'm not proud of all of them. Neither am I really ashamed of any of them. In some cases I might have been wrong. In no case was I insincere at the moment. Furthermore, I was always ready to apologize when I found out I had made a mistake or misjudged someone's intentions. I seldom had a serious quarrel with anyone. I get angry fast and yet I am not inclined to carry grudges. My basic quarrel was with those people—players, newsmen, and baseball big shots—who felt I had no right to assert myself simply because I was a black, and, being the first black in the game, ought to stay meek and mild forever. I had news for them. I hadn't come into baseball to try to be a great black baseball player. I had come into baseball to try to be a good player and, hopefully, to help people realize how silly it was to keep anyone out of the game because of the color of his skin.

I wasn't out to pick arguments. It was just that after two years of keeping quiet I had an awful lot stored up inside me. I had been going home at night, all keyed up, tense and irritable. I knew I wasn't going to be able to feel any relief until I could get some of the pressure off me, some of the tension out of my system. In the middle of 1948 the tension had started coming out.

Once during that season I had blown up, for the first time in my major league career, and was thrown out of a game. Umpire Butch Henline ruled me out of the game. Maybe you think I felt bad about being thrown out. Guess again! It made me feel good. This was normal. This was closer to being accepted, not as a black in base-ball, but just as a high-spirited ball-player. It also made me feel that baseball was growing up when a black player could be thrown out of a game with no one—including the player—thinking of race.

My new approach in 1949 brought on a lot of publicity. I'm not going to pretend that I don't like to see my name in the newspapers. Who in the public eye doesn't? On the other hand, I was constantly amazed when some of my most casual remarks to the umpire were blown up into major rhubarbs. Sometimes a newspaperman standing outside the dressing room would pick up my voice out of a chorus of protest by the Dodger team and blow it into a front-page ruckus. I also found myself in constant hot water because I refused to pull punches during radio and television or press interviews.

Whenever there was any rhubarb, it was to my cubicle that the writers came. Perhaps they didn't like the answers I gave to the questions they asked, but I think they knew they were honest answers and that I wouldn't back down and claim to be misquoted if a storm arose. They knew I would say what I believed.

One of the things I liked about 1949 was that I no longer fought a lonely, personal battle. I was fighting with and for our team. They had accepted me and my battles became theirs. We had all learned that working together and fighting for common goals as a unit is the winning technique. I knew that my team was behind me and that my fellow Dodgers would understand my motives in asserting myself.

Without a doubt, 1949 was my best season—the height of my baseball career. You can well believe that I didn't repeat my mistake of the year before, by neglecting my physical condition.

During the winter months I had worked at the YMCA in Harlem, helping the youngsters in that community to develop themselves and their bodies through the Y's splendid sports program.

When I checked in for spring training at Vero Beach, Florida, I was rested and relaxed. I had lost every trace of flabbiness.

Just as important as the condition of my body was the change in my state of mind. I was slowly but surely adjusting to be able to give—as well as take—according to whatever came along.

In spring training one of the rookies displayed a vicious streak as we were playing an intra-squad game. I suppose he figured that he could take out his frustrations on me and that I couldn't retaliate. I gave him a jolt. He made some insulting cracks and I gave them right back—with a little interest.

The intervention of the other players was the only thing that prevented a fight. This incident had repercussions later. Commissioner Chandler heard about it. He had also heard that I had made a statement to the effect that the people who had been picking on me had better not be rough on me in 1949 because I was going to be rough on them. I was summoned before Commissioner Chandler and reprimanded. That didn't bother me. But if people like Ty Cobb, Frankie Frisch, Pepper Martin, and others could be praised and looked upon as important to the game because they had natural reactions and let them be known, I figured I ought to get the same consideration.

It was this spirit which helped me to have a big year in 1949. Opening day at Ebbets Field brought out almost thirty-five thousand fans. We played the Giants. Gil Hodges was at first base and Campanella was catcher. Duke Snider held down center field. Reese and I were having the time of our lives as a double play combination.

During spring training Shotten had me hitting fourth.

By the end of May I was hitting .331, had six home runs, and led the league with thirty-four runs batted in.

I had to admit that Shotten had been right.

My fielding at second base and my teamwork with Reese combined to build my value to the team.

My top form didn't endear me to Durocher. Leo and I created several exciting episodes, throwing baseball-type insults back and forth. It was all in the teasing fun of competition. The funny part of it all was that we really respected each other deeply.

By June I was leading the league in batting with .348. The next month it was .350. That was the same month I nearly got into it with School-boy Rowe, the Phillies' pitcher. During a game Rowe kept shouting instructions to Philly men to knock me down.

In August the Cardinals were leading the

The most feared baserunner in the game, Robinson executes his trademark play—stealing home—against the Chicago Cubs.

league. We were in second position—a close, dangerous second.

I ran into bad luck in August, straining a ligament in my right foot. It was painful but I didn't dare quit then. My game fell off most of the month. We went to St. Louis to play a three-game series which could have been crucial in terms of the pennant.

From that day on, until the final day of the season, it was nip and tuck—so much so that on the final day we were still only one game ahead.

We won the final game of the season, 9–7. It was the second time in three years that the Dodgers had captured the National League pennant. We lost the Series to the Yankees again. However, I had made the National League All-Star team for the first time. I had a league-leading hitting average of .342. My percentage with men on bases was .360. I had 203 hits, 122 runs, 124 runs batted in, and had hit 16 home runs. I tied for the league lead in sacrifices and also led the league in stolen bases with thirty-seven. In the fall of the year sports writers voted me the Most Valuable Player Award.

In the annual All-Star game in July I was chosen to play second base for the National League.

As proud as I was to become the first black in the majors, the first to play in a World Series, the first to win the Most Valuable Player title, I was just as proud when a couple of honors came from interests outside of sports.

Sports magazine, the New York Uptown Chamber of Commerce, and the alumni of my old alma mater, UCLA, presented me with plaques and citations.

Mr. Rickey and I signed a 1950 contract for about $35,000. One could say Mr. Rickey's experiment had worked—also that it had paid off.

11

I Hang Up My Uniform

EARLY IN 1950 little Jackie, Jr., now three years old, was delighted to be able to tell everyone that he had a brand-new baby sister, Sharon.

The birth of my daughter gave me still another reason to continue to advance my position in baseball. I had a bad setback, however, as soon as the season opened. I twisted my left ankle in spring training. I decided to try to play with the ankle taped up. There wasn't much running I could do, but my batting was holding up until I collided with a catcher on the Giants' team and hurt my left knee. I couldn't even bend the leg and had to sit on the bench for three days. It was incredible how my luck was failing in those first few weeks. Soon after I was back on the field, I pulled a muscle in my left thigh. It wasn't bad enough to keep me from playing, but a few days later something else happened. I was hit in the left elbow, and it became inflamed. I had to move to seventh batting position for a while.

Whatever happened to me in 1950 happened on my left side. In September, playing the Phillies, I jammed my left thumb into the ground and was forced out of the game when it began swelling. I had torn some tendons in my hand. The team doctor put it in a splint. I was miserable for a week until I could substitute a rubber thumb protector for the splints and take back my old position at second base.

The 1950 season wasn't a terrific one for me. We didn't win the pennant. However, I came out of it with the fielding lead for the league's second baseman, a .986 average, and a National League record for double plays (153) by second basemen. I was chosen again for the All-Star team, had a hitting average of .328, fourteen home runs, and eighty-one batted in. My injuries prevented my running very much, so I had only twelve stolen bases.

A big cloud loomed on my horizon. Branch Rickey was leaving us, selling his interest to take over the Pittsburgh Pirates. I felt as if I were losing a father. He had been such a great inspiration to me. I wondered nervously how much his departure would affect my game and how I would make it with the front office in the future. I learned that Mr. O'Malley's feud with Mr. Rickey would have its effect on me.

Nothing happened immediately to justify my fears. Not too long after the change of ownership a situation arose which took my mind off Mr. Rickey's leaving—if only for a short time. While our team was in Cincinnati the local police and a newspaper received notes stating that I would be shot if I played at Crosley Field. It was the first time this kind of threat had been made since my first year in the majors. The FBI and police were stationed in strategic places at game time. Some of them were on guard on rooftops. Nothing ever came of the threats.

We lost the 1951 pennant to the Giants. But in the final game of the three-game playoff in Brooklyn, a piece of baseball history was made by the Giants' Bobby Thomson. In my opinion what happened ranks as one of the finest moments in the game. For six innings the score had remained 1–0, our favor. In the seventh the Giants tied the score, but at the bottom of the ninth we were leading 4–1. As far as most of the fans were concerned the pennant was ours, the game over. Some of the ardent Giant rooters even began leaving the stadium. In a last inning rally which left practically everyone dazed, Whitey Lockman doubled to left field. Dark scored and Mueller made it to third. The score was now 4–2. Tying runs were on the bases. Bobby Thomson came to the plate. Charley Dressen benched Don New-combe and sent in Ralph Branca. Thomson swung and the crowd went mad as the ball went into the left field stands to give the Giants the pennant.

It took a couple of years after that Series before I found out how different things were going to be with Mr. Rickey gone.

My first trouble came during spring training in Miami. I had been injured and was unable to play in exhibition games. O'Malley sent for me.

"I don't like your missing these exhibition games," he told me. "The fans want to see you play. It's not fair to them for you to be out of the lineup.

"Furthermore," he continued, "I've had re-ports that you've been complaining about having to stay in a separate hotel in Miami. That was good enough for you in 1947. Why do you have to make trouble now?"

Rae was with me. I think both of us found it hard to believe what we were hearing. After all that had been accomplished to prove that a black had a right to be in the majors and that he could be successful and bring more money into the game, here was a man who was asking us to be satisfied with things as they used to be.

"I took a lot of things in 1947," I pointed out.

''I didn't take them because I felt that they were 'good enough' for me. I had to go along in order to prove an important point. I happen to feel now, however, that there are a lot of insults being suffered by Negro ballplayers that wouldn't be necessary if the owners would show a bit more courage.''

I added that, as for my absence from the exhibition games, no one could truthfully accuse me of lying down on the job or giving less than my best for the team. My injuries were genuine and could be checked out. I was staying out of the exhibition games to make sure I would be in top physical shape for the coming season. I considered this more important than taking a chance on aggravating an injury in an exhibition game.

Rae usually has little to say when other people are discussing business. She seldom displays temper, but O'Malley's accusation got to her.

''Mr. O'Malley,'' she snapped, ''I feel I must say a few words here. Of all the things Jackie Robinson is, the one thing he is not is a prima donna. I've seen him play with sore legs, a sore back, sore arms, even without other members of the team knowing it, doing it not for praise but because he was always thinking about the team. Nobody worries more about this club more than Jackie Robinson, Mr. O'Malley, and I say that includes the owners. I live with him, so I know. I've watched him getting up early in the morning to look out the window to see what kind of day it's going to be—if it's going to be good weather for the game, if the team is likely to have a good crowd. Nobody else spends more time worrying about Pee Wee Reese's sore foot or Gil Hodges' batting slump or Carl Erskine's ailing arm, and I want you to know that it pains me deeply to have you say what you just said.''

Rae went on to say that bringing me into the majors was not the greatest thing Branch Rickey ever did. The greatest thing, she said, was the way he stuck by me.

''He understood Jack. He never listened to ugly little rumors such as you mentioned to us today. Mr. Rickey ignored such rumors completely. If there was something wrong, or if he heard there was something wrong, he would go to Jackie and ask him, 'Is this so?' or 'Are you unhappy about this, Jack?' He would talk to Jack and they would get to the heart of it like men with a mutual respect for each other's abilities and feelings.''

Rae was really magnificent that day. In fact, she inspired me to go even further than I had intended in answering O'Malley. I told him that not only was it true that I resented our Jim Crow hotel accommodations, but I also resented the fact that whoever had made arrangements had picked such a crummy place. There were no adjoining rooms. Rae and I were forced to sleep across the hall from our two small children. This meant we couldn't hear them if they awoke during the night.

"It doesn't strike me too well to have people who sit in comfort in an air-conditioned hotel lecture to me about not complaining about where I live," I told O'Malley.

"No harm meant," he said, "but won't you just try—won't you just try to come out and play today?"

We agreed that I would play that day.

In 1954 Walter Alston succeeded Chuck Dressen as manager. Alston was a nice man, quiet and decent. But some of us on the team felt he lacked confidence and that because of this he was given to making some very unwise decisions and judgments in the heat of play. Gradually tension began to build between Alston and me. One factor which brought this on was Alston's conviction that I resented his replacing my good friend Chuck Dressen. However, there wasn't any surface trouble between Walt and me in 1954, even though there were real barriers which separated us. As I look back on that situation, I deeply regret that I didn't sit down and talk with Walt, man to man. I firmly believe that had I done so, we could have resolved our differences.

Those differences came to a head toward the end of the season. On several occasions I allowed my building resistance to Walt to show and made angry remarks which might have been better left unsaid.

At Wrigley Field in Chicago, that season, Duke Snider hit a ball into the left-field seats. The ball appeared to hit a spectator. The rules stipulated that a ball like this which cleared the wall was an automatic home run. If interfered with by a spectator in the field of play, it became a two-bagger. Umpire Bill Stewart assumed that the ball had bounced off the wall. He ruled it a double. I ran from the dugout to register my objection. I thought that other members of the team were following me. I didn't realize that I was alone. Alston stood at third base, his hands on his hips, staring at me as if to say: "All right, Robinson, all the fans see you. Cut out the grandstand tactics and get back to the dugout." I felt like a fool. I knew this embarrassing situation would fit with all the rumors that I was a hot head—the guy always eager to rush out and argue with the umpires when no one else seemed to feel there was anything to argue about. I mumbled a few words to the umpire and walked off the field. I was furious. In the dugout someone made matters worse by teasing me.

"You should have heard what Walt said when you were out on the field, Jack."

That was all I needed.

"If that guy didn't stand out there at third base like a wooden Indian," I retorted, "this club might go somewhere. Here's a play that meant a run in a tight ball game, so whether I was right or wrong, the play was close enough for him to protest to the umpire. But not Alston. What kind of manager is that?"

The next day the newspapers carried a picture of the fan who had been struck by the ball. The picture proved beyond all doubt that the play had been a home run.

It was during 1955 that I began to think of leaving baseball. I had put in ten good years. For some time I had been beset by growing fears about what was going to happen to me when I hung up my uniform. I realized that baseball wasn't ready to accept a black on an administrative level. I had little chance of becoming a manager or being placed in some other executive position.

I was sure that O'Malley wanted me out of the

Dodgers. There was a rumor that a young player, Don Hoak, would be considered for my job—then on third base.

More than anything, I dreaded getting benched frequently and having to sit on the sidelines from day to day. This very thing began to happen in 1955. Alston had me in the lineup one day and the next day on the bench. This is the way a ballplayer loses his timing and becomes rusty.

In Knoxville, Tennessee, at an exhibition game I sat on the bench. I should have gone to Walt Alston privately and had it out with him. Instead I made the mistake of asking a newspaperman, Dick Young of the New York *Daily News*, if he had heard whether I was going to play that season. I knew the sportswriters often got off-the-record tips from the front office. Dick said he hadn't heard anything and questioned me closely about my doubts. Alston learned about this conversation and boiled over. He called a meeting of the team and without mentioning my name blasted "players who run to newspapermen with their problems."

Alston seemed determined to provoke me into a quarrel. Finally he made the statement: "And another thing—this business of players going around shooting off their mouths about who's a wooden Indian and all that stuff, that's the kind of business that's got to go.''

I had had it. I sounded off angrily and Walt and I began shouting at each other. The argument could have developed into a fight if it hadn't been for Gil Hodges who kept tapping me on the arm and telling me to cool down. I respected Gil and finally took his advice.

To further inflame the situation, the press began getting on Walt's back about my absence from the lineup. He was harassed unmercifully. I am sure now that I didn't appreciate, as I should have, the difficult position Walt was in.

That whole season turned out to be a pretty bad one for me. Being benched so often, I had lost my sharpness. I hit only .256 and had driven in a measly thirty-six runs. My fielding was off. My average was .966 compared to the .992 with which I had set an all-time second baseman record in 1951. I had played in eighty-four games at third, ten at outfield, and one each at first base and second base. I was aware that, as baseball years go, I was getting old.

With my miserable record in 1955 and all the problems about the future on my mind, I certainly didn't expect the miracle which happened that year in the Series. Here's the way a Milwaukee *Journal* sports writer described the Series game which set the stage for the miracle:

> A creaky old man of thirty-six convinced the Brooklyn Dodgers Friday that they can beat the hated New York Yankees after all.
>
> Jackie Robinson, forgetting for this day, at least, about the silver in his hair and the age in his legs, rallied the Dodgers almost single-handedly from the coma that had gripped them the first two days of baseball's World Series. He batted and fielded and ran them to an 8–3 victory as 34,209 fans yelled themselves hoarse.
>
> Technically, it was Johnny Podres who beat the Yanks. The youthful lefty, by way of celebrating his twenty-third birthday, pitched a strong seven-hitter and struck out six. Actually, however, the guy who did the job was Robinson, the one Dodger who everybody was sure was nearing the end of the major league line.

There were more instances during that Series when I got major credit for pulling our team through to victory. It was one of the most exciting episodes in baseball history. We beat the Yankees four games to three.

One December day in 1956 I told Rae that my mind was made up. I was going to retire from baseball. Having heard this announcement a number of times, she nodded cautiously. I don't believe she thought I really meant it, but I did. Just when my worry about the future had reached

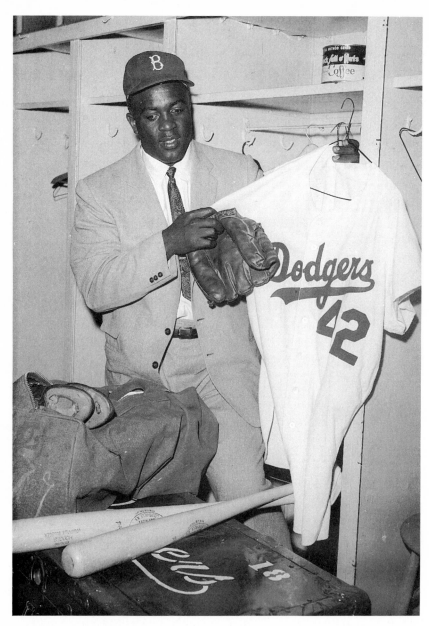

After a brilliant ten-year career, Robinson retired from baseball after the 1956 season. Moving into the business world, he became vice-president of the Chock Full O' Nuts Company.

its peak, I received a call from Dave Alber, the publicity man with Chock Full O'Nuts, a restaurant chain. This call set in motion the events which ended in my signing with that company for an executive job. It was more than another job, however. From the career of baseball, I would be making the transition into the world of business.

12

It's the Next Decision That Counts

ACROSS THE GLASS WINDOW of my television set—on a spring afternoon—I see our nation's favorite sport played out with all its thrills and drama. It is unusual today to see a major league team that doesn't have black players. We haven't rid ourselves of all prejudice in sports, but we are moving ahead. Sometimes I think that is what democracy means, the process of constantly moving ahead.

There are many things I reminisce about these days. One of them is how important spring training is in the career of a player. I believe youth can be compared to the spring training period of our lives. When I was with the Dodgers and we were in spring training, we knew that what we did in those six weeks would have a tremendous effect on what we would be able to accomplish in the six months ahead. We took our spring training responsibilities very seriously. I have always contended that this was the reason the Brooklyn ball club was so successful.

When I see young people breaking the training rules, I believe they are doing it because they have little faith in themselves and their ability. It seems they have said to themselves: "What's the use? I'll never be what I want to be or accomplish what I want to do. I might as well enjoy myself while I am young."

They see other youngsters who are so far ahead of them in progress in school. They see others who are captains of football and soccer teams or presidents of debating societies. Or they might see youngsters who seem to have so much more than they have—clothes, money, a car.

So they give up. They give up because the road ahead seems so long and winding and almost impossible to travel.

The trick is to learn to accept defeats, small ones and big ones. Learn while you are still young and you will be prepared for the major setbacks which you might have to meet in later life. I've known some fine winners in the sports world. I've also known some wonderful losers. Sometimes the winners faded. The good losers never did stay down.

I guess it all boils down to the need to have

faith in yourself and to learn to appreciate other people in whom you can have faith. One thing is certain. You cannot make it alone in life.

I'll never regret the faith I placed in Branch Rickey. He showed such real faith in me. Another thing that impressed me was the deep faith he had in God.

Some people have laughed at this grand old man because he is so dramatic and so outspoken in his religious convictions. Others have insinuated that he is not sincere because he speaks so frequently and so emotionally about the Fatherhood of God and the brotherhood of man.

I am not one of the big people in terms of faith. But I would have to be pretty stupid, and certainly ungrateful, not to have had some of the deep religious conviction of my mother, Mallie Robinson, and Mr. Rickey rub off on me.

When I was born in January, 1919, in the bedroom of a small farm close to Cairo, Georgia, it is said that my mother, holding me in her arms and looking about her at the poverty of our home, whispered: "Bless you, boy. For you to survive all this, God will have to keep His eye on you."

More than thirty years later, Branch Rickey said: "Surely, God was with me when I picked Jackie Robinson as the first Negro player in the major leagues."

I don't go around wearing religion on my

sleeve. I believe in God, in the Bible, and in trying to do the right thing as I understand it. I am certain there are many better Christians than I. Yet it has always impressed me that two of the people who had the greatest influence on my life—Mallie Robinson and Branch Rickey—had in common such strong faith in the existence of a Supreme Being. It is one thing to express faith verbally. It is another thing to practice your beliefs daily as these two people did.

Most baseball executives considered it in the line of duty when they had to work or attend games on Sundays. I was surprised to learn that the Dodger boss stayed away from the ball park on Sundays because of his religious belief. Mr. Rickey once told me about the promise he made to God and to himself when he was teaching sports at college. He promised that if he succeeded in becoming a power in baseball, he would dedicate himself to breaking down the barriers which kept black players out of the major leagues.

He was able to do such a good job of destroying these barriers because he believed in what he was doing. In my opinion people, young or old, ought to stick to and have the courage to express the things in which they believe.

On a television show once, a girl asked me whether I believed the New York Yankees team was discriminating against blacks. I had believed this to be true for a long time. I said exactly what I thought. I said the ballplayers on the Yankee club held no anti-black prejudice, as far as I knew. As for the management of the club, I felt they were anti-black.

The following morning, headlines announced that I had accused the Yankees of prejudice. The Yankees denied it. The sports writers had a bazaar. I was called a soapbox orator and a few other names. So much attention was created by the newspapers that Commissioner Ford Frick summoned me to his office.

I had decided that I would be completely honest with the commissioner. After he and I had exchanged pleasantries, I went straight to the point.

I told Commissioner Frick that if I had been called in because of my statement about the Yankees, I might as well be frank. If someone had asked me the same question the next day, I would have given the same answer. I said I made the statement only after things I had learned over a period of years about the Yankees. I said that no one was going to deprive me of my right, as a private citizen, to say whatever I believed about racial discrimination.

I also suggested that the commissioner get a transcript of the television program to compare what I had actually said with the tremendous production created in the papers.

Commissioner Frick's reaction was positive. I fully understood his position as baseball's commissioner, but I also had added respect for him as a man when he said, "Jack, I just want you to know how I feel personally about this thing. Whenever you believe enough in something to sound off about it, whenever you feel, deep in your heart, that you have got to come out swinging, I sincerely hope that you'll swing the real heavy bat and not the fungo."

A newspaperman once tried to prove to me that my habit of sounding off had been pretty costly to me.

"Don't you know that sports writers, in the main, don't approve of this kind of thing?" he argued. "Remember, we are the ones who nominate you guys for awards."

I have a room full of trophies and awards in our home. This newspaperman was telling me I had lost some pretty important awards which I might have received on the basis of achievement if I had only been willing to keep my mouth shut.

Now, I love awards. Who doesn't? But what good is a trophy or an award you get for being silent when your conscience tells you you ought to speak out?

Just as I received a lot of criticism for living out

this belief in baseball, I've also antagonized a lot of people, not only of the white race, but also some of my own, for applying the same principle to my participation in civil rights after leaving baseball.

I've toured the country making speeches, helping to raise funds, and writing articles for the National Association for the Advancement of Colored People. People have said to me, "Why should you do this? You've got a nice home, a good job. You've got no beef. Life has been wonderful to you. This civil rights problem is for civil rights leaders. It isn't any of your business."

Well, I just happen to believe that American democracy is the business of every American. The NAACP has done a wonderful job, not only in the interest of blacks, but in the interest of American democracy. There's another reason I feel so strongly about the NAACP. That organization was right out in front in the fight to get recognition in baseball for black youngsters. If I were to turn my back on an organization of this kind or refuse to aid its progress, I would be a pretty ungrateful person.

When I think about this struggle for equal opportunity for all of us Americans, it reminds me of the way I have always felt about arguing with the umpire. They used to call me an umpire baiter. Let me tell you something about ball-players and umpires. I've often heard it said: ''It never does any good to protest to umpires. They never change their decisions.''

As far as it goes, that observation is correct. Professional players realize that umpires rarely reverse a decision no matter how much you pro-test. Still, we used to squawk for all we were worth when we thought a ruling was unfair. We were not really protesting in the hope of having any change made about the particular play at issue. On that point, we would have been fighting a lost cause.

It was the next play, the next decision, that counted.

If the next play was close and could be called either way, nine out of ten times the player who didn't believe in protesting would have the play called against him.

Umpires are human too. They don't want to lose favor with home town fans. When the play is close, they instinctively favor the guy who has a tendency to open his big mouth and holler for his rights.

That's the way I feel about the civil rights situa-tion in this country. If the fans—the public—see you walk away from a raw decision as if you don't care, they won't want to root for you to win. If

*Robinson (followed by the Rev. Martin Luther King, Jr.) re-
ceived an honorary degree from Howard University in June
1957. He died on October 24, 1972, twenty-five years after
breaking major league baseball's "color line."*

you don't care, they won't. That's why I refuse to run into a dugout of unconcern about what happens to my fellow Americans.

I want the right side to win the next decision.

For Further Reading

Davidson, Margaret. *The Story of Jackie Robinson*. New York: Dell, 1988.

Epstein, Sam and Beryl. *Jackie Robinson*. New York: Garrard, 1974.

Frommer, Harvey. *Jackie Robinson*. New York: Franklin Watts, 1984.

Scott, Richard. *Jackie Robinson*. New York: Chelsea House, 1987.

Index